MW00989949

Once again Joe Battaglia h
Unfriended, to explore another crucial piece of what makes us
human. He studies an extremely complex issue that faces us
today, one that has no simple answers. We all know the power
of social media—the entire world of computers, smartphones,
and little boxes that answer questions for us when called upon.
Often, lives are saved and true change is brought forth with
their invention. But like so many things, there is a dark side to
technological achievement that lingers and threatens. Are we
capable of knowing where the line begins and ends in our reliance
on it? Which, of course, leads to the greater question, do we have
the moral foundation to know where this line even is? The answer
to this is yes! God has drawn that line quite clearly and placed it
in each of our hearts. But what if we're already "too far gone" by
the very thing itself—by social media and its ability to disconnect
as readily as connect—to reach within ourselves and know where
to begin looking? This is all heavy stuff, but in the hands of Joe, a
friend I will never "unfriend," he lays it all out as only he can do in
simple and easy servings that shed needed light.

—CORBIN BERNSEN, producer, director, and actor
in *L.A. Law*, *Major League*, and *Psych*

What a timely book! What wisdom, insight, and clarity! And
what a doable and necessary plan to change the world, or at least
our part in it. *Unfriended* is a powerful, practical, necessary, and
needed book. But more than that, Joe Battaglia is my friend who
lives what he teaches. He's the real deal, and one should always
trust words from someone who does more than preach. Read this
book and give it to everyone you know!

—DR. STEVE BROWN, author, host of Key Life Radio Network

My friend Joe Battaglia, in his new book *Unfriended*, aims squarely
and hits the target about what's really at the core of much of our

societal angst in a social-media-driven culture—the hunger in our hearts for real community. We've been looking for love in all the wrong places, and Joe points us back in the right direction to describe what we are all hardwired for—a meaningful relationship with God and each other.

—RITA COSBY, Emmy-winning TV and radio host,
bestselling author

Joe Battaglia's insights about the value we find when we get face-to-face and intersect with others will have you rethinking your social-media time and reconnecting with those around you. Using research and reasoning, he shows us that stepping out of the anonymity of the social-media world and stepping into the lives of others to find community is the only way healing, hope, and purpose can be found and truly shared in our world. Joe's writing is both thought provoking and practical, guiding us in how we can "unfriend" not only to change our habits but also the way we approach each day. In *Unfriended*, he shows us how Jesus intended for us to live in community.

—KIM CRABILL,
founder/director of ROSESANDRAINBOWS.org

Much of what we hear and see in our news today is about darkness, fear, and disillusionment. Our world has become so distracted and disconnected that we've lost our way in our relationships with each other. Some turn to social media to try to find hope, but a phone or a tablet is a poor substitute for another human being who will bring you light and love in your life. In *Unfriended*, my dear friend Joe Battaglia gently reminds us how vital true community is more now than ever, and offers some practical and unique insights into how we can recover what our hearts so desperately need. Read it for the good of your soul.

—ROMA DOWNEY, actor, producer,
New York Times bestselling author

The greatest commandments are love God and love your neighbor. In *Unfriended*, Joe Battaglia provides a blueprint to share the love of God by joyfully and purposefully engaging in a loving community.

— STEVE FEDYSKI, COO, Pure Flix Entertainment

My dear friend Joe Battaglia is calling for true community and a connection with God in his new book, *Unfriended*. In a society that heavily depends on social media to build up self-esteem and develop relationships, his book is not only necessary, but urgent. I recommend everyone put down their phones and pick up this book. You will be changed!

—DEVON FRANKLIN, producer and *New York Times* bestselling author

It seems like we're angry all the time. And we're losing our way in how to establish true relationships. My friend Joe Battaglia has written a beautiful book, *Unfriended*, that points us in the proper direction to restore true community in our ever-challenging time. Joe changes the way we look at the world—and ourselves.

—MIKE GALLAGHER, host of *The Mike Gallagher Show*, Salem Radio Network, New York

My friend, Joe Battaglia, has written a profoundly important book that uniquely encapsulates the growing national addiction to social media. He not only analyzes the current problems this generation is facing; he offers solutions too. This book is a powerful tool for understanding and navigating.

—KATHIE LEE GIFFORD, co-host of the fourth hour of *Today* and the *New York Times* bestselling book *The Rock, the Road, and the Rabbi*

Information is a game changer and affects our choices. What if the road we initially imagined taking us toward our desired destination of "community" was, in fact, taking us in the opposite direction? Joe Battaglia's book *Unfriended* explores social media and its impact on our deep longing for true community. It's the timely read we need.

— A<small>MY</small> G<small>RANT</small>, singer/songwriter

In an era in which we have more tools than ever before to make us more "social," humanity is remarkably the least social it has been in generations. Human beings were built for community, yet increased incivility and social chaos have made achieving true interaction increasingly difficult. Meanwhile, intolerance abounds. Joe Battaglia perfectly illustrates the problem and shows us what's at stake if we don't turn a corner—and fast. Truly an amazing book.

—B<small>ILLY</small> H<small>ALLOWELL</small>, author of Fault Line
and The Armageddon Code

Unfriended is a book that needed to be written, and I'm glad Joe Battaglia is the one who wrote it. We live in a deeply disconnected culture, and we're not made to live like this. We're yearning for so much more. This book acknowledges our brokenness and how annoying we humans can be. Then it proposes that we love each other anyway. It's counter-cultural, plain spoken, and thoroughly refreshing.

—B<small>RANT</small> H<small>ANSEN</small>, radio host of "The Brant Hansen Show," and
author of Unoffendable and Blessed Are the Misfits

"Must read" is thrown around—a lot. But here I am using it very intentionally. You must read Unfriended if you are a parent of a child under eighteen, and you ought to read it if you or anyone you love is using social media, which is just about everyone. Joe Battaglia has penned a cri de coeur about the poisons that have escaped into our world via the new platforms for connecting but not communicating, the acid on the soul that accompanies every technological advance, and the desperately needed solutions to the online chaos surrounding each and every one of us. Whether you agree with me or "hate" me because of my positions on television, radio, or the Web, trust me on this: Joe Battaglia—this son of immigrants, this long-serving, widely admired marketing professional and sincerely devoted follower of Jesus has a word for you—one you need as I did and as everyone does.

—HUGH HEWITT, host with the Salem Radio Network and *MSNBC, Washington Post* columnist, *New York Times* bestselling author, and Professor of Law at Chapman University Fowler School of Law

In a world where *friend* has become a verb, and being unfriended is little more than a click away, in his new book, Joe Battaglia shares with us how much real community means and how we can rebuild and maintain relationships with our neighbors, our friends, our family, and, most importantly, with God, our Creator. It is a wonderful trek through fond memories of how it used to be before the onslaught of social media and fake news, but Joe also offers real, practical solutions about connecting one-on-one and about sharing a common bond that unites us more than divides us! You will enjoy reading this remarkable perspective on relationships and building true community!

—JACKELYN VIERA ILOFF, author of *What If You Could?* and senior advisor at Joel Osteen Ministries

Joe, thanks for reminding us of the need for real, face-to-face community instead of superficial, social-media connections. Your practical, biblical insights are spot-on.

—ALEX KENDRICK, filmmaker of *Fireproof, Courageous,* and *War Room*

Unfriended: an outrageously important must-read! Joe Battaglia's critically important work has the audacity to call out and define one of, if not the most untouchable, glaring weaknesses in society and do this simultaneously with a genuinely caring heart that gently pushes us toward a most practical solution.

—KEVIN MCCULLOUGH, author, Fox News commentator, and nationally syndicated host of "The Kevin McCullough" show

In a culture geared toward self-absorption, Joe Battaglia offers an important reminder that God made us for one another. *Unfriended* will challenge you to show the same love and sacrifice for others that Jesus did for us!

—JANET MEFFERD, host of *Janet Mefferd Today* and *Janet Mefferd Live*

True community has never been more important than it is now, so I salute my dear friend Joe Battaglia for presciently assembling these tremendous reflections on that very subject. May we all read them with joy and become part of the solution to this supremely vital aspect of our lives.

—ERIC METAXAS, *New York Times* bestselling author of *Bonhoeffer, Miracles, If You Can Keep It,* and *Martin Luther*

In *Unfriended*, Joe Battaglia gives us fresh insights into what *really* may be lacking in our culture today that has led to a loss of the true sense of community we once enjoyed. We need to regain what we've lost and stop listening to the false prophets who have hijacked our national narrative of how we should think, feel, and respond to each other. This book will make you think. And it will speak to your heart as well. I highly recommend it!

—KEVIN SORBO, producer, actor, *Hercules: The Legendary Journeys, Andromeda, Soul Surfer, God's Not Dead,* and *Let There Be Light*

This is an important book. We are living in a day where we are more "connected" than ever yet more alone. True community is worth fighting for, and Joe shows us how to do it.

—SHEILA WALSH, author, speaker

Unfriended

Finding TRUE
COMMUNITY
in a DISCONNECTED
CULTURE

JOE BATTAGLIA

BroadStreet
PUBLISHING

BroadStreet Publishing® Group, LLC
Savage, Minnesota, USA
BroadStreetPublishing.com

Unfriended: Finding True Community in a Disconnected Culture

Copyright © 2018 Joe Battaglia

978-1-4245-5732-5 (softcover)
978-1-4245-5733-2 (e-book)

Stock or custom editions of BroadStreet Publishing titles may be purchased in bulk for educational, business, ministry, fundraising, or sales promotional use. For information, please email info@broadstreetpublishing.com.

Interior design and typesetting by Katherine Lloyd at theDESKonline.com
Cover design by Chris Garborg at garborgdesign.com

Printed in the United States of America

18 19 20 21 22 5 4 3 2 1

To my wife LuAnn ... of almost thirty-seven years. Until God decided to call her back to His community ahead of the schedule I would have preferred.

Her infectious smile was her trademark. When you were around her, it was all about you. Our contentious, self-aggrandizing world needs more LuAnns. People wanted to be around her. And that is a mark of greatness … changing the world without changing yourself.

She embodied the kind of community I describe in this book, and wish for everyone.

If I listen closely enough, I can still hear her calling my name.

Heaven may be closer than we think.

Contents

Foreword

By Todd Starnes

M r. Rogers asked a question at the beginning of his iconic
children's television program: "Won't you be my neighbor?"
It was a simple song with a profound message—a message about
community, about friendship. And it struck a chord with young-
sters taking those first steps into building a social network.

But today Mr. Roger's neighborhood is anything but sociable
or friendly, thanks in large part to social media. We live in an
age where our self-worth is determined by Facebook "likes" and
Instagram "hearts." Careers and friendships can be ended in 280
characters or less. The social networks that were meant to bring
us together have in fact made us less sociable. We have become
a nation in search of community.

Joe Battaglia does a masterful job addressing these issues
in *Unfriended*. And he puts us on the right path to finding true
community: "Social media may establish a form of communication, but it cannot establish true community," Joe tells us.

Unfriended is a deep dive into simple truths that can foster
a community that will make a difference and impact lives for

the kingdom. Along the way, Joe compels us to "unfriend" bad habits that might set up roadblocks to building community— from scapegoating to political wrangling. This book is not for the fainthearted. Joe tackles political correctness and the cultural morass that has infested our nation. And he challenges us to engage in a bit of spiritual soul searching.

All that to say, Joe has crafted a terrific book that explores a fascinating topic—how to discover true community, true friendship, by being "unfriended."

—Todd Starnes, *Fox News*

"One from Many"

THE MOTTO OF COMMUNITY

nscribed on the back of every coin are the Latin words *E pluribus unum*. That may be all someone ever sees of Latin nowadays. I suspect that most Americans know the phrase means "one from many." The heterogeneous makeup of our population has long represented our nation's genius in that we are one nation formed from many different people.

Simply, we are all different yet one. Not that we are all the same and one.

There is a reason why this simple phrase embodies America's greatness, regardless of the historical revisionists, who would rewrite much about our history simply because they are either ignorant of facts or prefer to overlay their modern-day perspectives on anything that happened many years ago that does not fit their current agendas.

The wonder of the "one from many" motto was instilled in me very early in my life as the son of immigrants. My parents were born in Italy, immigrated to America in the 1930s, and never went back. My paternal grandparents lived with us as well, reinforcing the appreciation of my roots *and* their perspectives of the privilege of being an American. Those two sentiments were never held in tension in my family. They represented the two sides of a coin of the strength of our nation.

Unfortunately, much of our current national narrative seems to have forgotten that our strength lies in our differences—and our ability to see beyond differences for the greater good.

My father was not quite seventeen when he came to America. As such, he had vivid memories of his childhood and young adulthood in Italy, living in a small mountain town in Calabria in clear sight of the sea about eight miles down the mountain. He would tell me about his idyllic life as a child, especially during the summer months, when he and his friends would walk down the mountain and spend several days at the beach without coming home. He'd take some salami and cheese from the cellar, catch fish in the sea, and sleep under the stars on the beach. They were self-sufficient because they grew or raised everything they needed. It was their version of Mayberry. It sounded so good.

But then he would tell me stories of how hard it was in the winter when he got here to America, especially working during the Depression, how he had to go without a coat one winter because he could not afford one, and how my grandfather would get up at four a.m. to walk five miles to a neighboring town to get to work at six. I asked why he didn't take a bus. Simple. They always walked in Italy, and it was easier on flat land with sidewalks than in the mountains. Plus, you saved the five cents it cost for the bus ride and bought some food with that nickel. Oh.

So I asked him one day why even come to America and face the hardships of living in a foreign environment—start all over, work into the evening, and all the other things that accompany an immigrant's new life in a new land.

And his answer was simple. First, they could sense that war was coming in Europe. Plus, America was the land of opportunity. It afforded a person, through their hard work, what luxury and ease cannot afford a person—identity and self-realization. You see, there is something within the heart of each of us that yearns to realize what we are wired to be and do—and then to be free to do it.

That heartfelt yearning is exemplified best in these stirring lines of the Declaration of Independence: "We hold these truths to be self-evident, that all men are created equal, that they endowed by their Creator with certain unalienable Rights, that among these are Life, Liberty and the pursuit of Happiness."[1]

The great experiment in establishing a new nation was based upon the understanding that since "all men are created equal" and in God's image, people can coexist *if* they remain glued to that fact. This one principle was understood to be naturally observed and foundational to the universe working in sync with the Creator.

Inherent to our national motto is an understanding of the greatness of plurality and the necessity of having people who are different from each other speak into each other's lives. We can only act upon this if indeed we believe that we are made in God's image and are therefore equal. All of us. Everyone.

America was founded upon the realization that we *must* have differences to be more fully one. The universal principle to that is clearly evident by the diversity exhibited in creation. No two snowflakes are alike. Identical twins are not even identical. God's creation is manifest in such a way that differences actually create similarities. Or they should.

America was founded upon the realization that we must have differences to be more fully one.

When differences come together in an appreciation of people's God-given opportunities, the resultant outcome is strength, not weakness. Just the opposite of what many seem to think.

Part of the issue we face today is the lack of appreciation of our differences. It's easy to hide within so-called online communities of sameness. And then we bemoan the problems in our world caused by those who think differently, act differently, or look differently from us.

We all cannot, and should not, believe the same way or even the same things. Sameness and similarity do not enhance people's ability to come together; instead, differences actually contribute to establishing oneness as they fill in the gaps left by sameness. When we lose sight of that, intolerance grows.

Those who only want to be with "their own" must be the loneliest people around. It's so easy to bash the straw men we create to blame for all the ills in our world. In the end, we are the ones who suffer from the ills of sameness.

This is what we see happening today as politically correct agendas are foisting the notion of sameness upon people. Everyone *must* agree on every new cultural aberration or type of behavior or risk being labeled as intolerant. The hypocrisy of that statement is blatantly obvious, yet many fail to see it. As a result, the prevailing mind-set today is "us versus them," which we see played out so dramatically in our culture. This mentality is so disastrous to oneness because it prevents true intersection in life.

We get along best when we have to interact with each other and rely on each other for our sustenance. I am much more likely to get to know you, appreciate you, and even befriend you when I'm sweating alongside you for a common goal. I may even learn from you and appreciate things I would never be confronted with unless I heard your voice, listened to what you said, and sensed the hope in your soul, which sounds a lot like my heart and soul.

You can't get that in an online "community" or in believing like everyone else. It's the way the universe operates. There is no adequate substitute for looking into your eyes to see eternity in your soul and to hear the heartbeat of your dream.

So it brings us back to my father's idyllic life in that small, nondescript Italian mountainside town. Why leave Shangri-La for potential hardship, sweat, and uncomfortable surroundings? Why leave behind one's family to live among strangers?

Simple. It's the way we're wired and what makes the human family spin. Community fulfills the longing in our hearts and souls for differences that will complete us. Not the same things that only make us stale. And boring.

And if there's one thing the universe is *not*, it's boring!

Is it time to hang around with those different from you? Unfriend the mind-set of sameness, as well as the mistaken notion that you'll find security in being with people just like you. You aren't really safe. Get in the game and find out what you were really meant to be and do. You only find that in a community of "one from many."

2

Roots

THE FOUNDATION OF COMMUNITY

If you happen to take a short drive north of San Francisco, you'll run into one of the great natural treasures of our country, the California redwood forest. The sizes of those coniferous trees are legendary and stunning. It's hard to imagine that one of those trees grew from some little seed.

You would think that the very size of those redwoods would dictate that each one must have a huge underground root system to keep it from toppling over during a major storm. To the contrary; they have a very shallow root system. The one thing that saves the trees from falling is that the root systems become so intertwined that all the trees are connected as a group to support each individual one.

Now that sounds like a real community. It's all about the roots. A strong foundation with connections to others enhances the overall strength of a community to help everyone withstand whatever forces are thrown against it. That's why nature does not create a fully grown tree. A tree's growth period allows it to establish a foundation of roots to weather storms and give it stability, shelter other creatures, and serve as a witness to God's presence.

We are much like those trees.

The strength to sustain ourselves against the forces in life that seek to topple us is only found in community. The living of life in real time and in context of each other's lives gives us stability, meaning, identity, and love. These are the roots that form a very solid system of interdependence with other members of the community. This is the model that has worked throughout history.

When we seek to live virtually, none of these characteristics are ours to share. Or even to experience. Those who rely on social media as their community are relying on an environment that was not meant to provide it and is incapable of being it. Simply, the physical intertwining of our roots is impossible in a virtual context.

So those who have substituted this artificial community for the real one and then expect to receive from it all the things you receive from a real community will awaken one day only to find the emptiness of artificial satisfaction. As a result, we get confused as to what we can expect from our virtual world. We have believed the lie, and like all lies, it leads us into a dead end of human experience.

Unfortunately, people have not only begun living in this artificial community, but they have also built their homes on this foundation, expecting to find fulfillment that cannot be achieved. Ultimately, the more people spend time in an artificial "community," the more likely they will topple when forces come against them. Often, their purpose in life will topple as well.

And if we have no purpose, the logical next step in someone's mind could be that neither does anyone else have purpose. Daily, we see this mind-set acted out in random acts of rage, suicide, or anger. These acts are often the response of the logical conclusion that comes to many, namely, that they don't matter. And if they don't matter, they might even decide that other people don't matter either.

So if they don't matter, and if other people don't matter, and there is no true community they are part of to offset that way of thinking, then they can come to the conclusion that they can walk into a school or restaurant or theater and randomly take lives. Society then looks for a "reason" for such random violence and can only point to mental illness or the availability of guns.

The real answer is much deeper than that, but our politically correct culture refuses to address those issues because they do not fit into the box we've built to keep out the discussion about absolute truth. Or truth beyond ourselves.

If there is no absolute truth to which we are accountable, you might reason that there's no absolute standard for right or wrong as well. In that case, a Bernie Madoff or anyone else can create intricate models of deception to rob people of their life savings and ruin their lives.

We have looked everywhere for possible answers to the way in which our society has seemingly imploded with rage, lack of civility, corruption, and open and outright disregard for others. Could it be that the absence of true community is the answer? This artificial community has created such distortion as to the inherent value of others that there is no longer any inhibition to protecting those values. To the Christ-follower, though, there is an answer, and there is an objective reality to truth. Jesus embodied true community. He still calls us today to follow His model for community, which is the sharing of life in common. The communists and the utopian socialists had it all wrong. It was never about sharing goods and services; it was always about sharing each other.

Community started as the Trinity before creation and continues to this day. Notice that God used plural pronouns in Genesis 1:16: "Let *us* make mankind in *our* image, in *our* likeness" (emphasis added). He created the earth and the human race for a distinct purpose: to exhibit His glory and have fellowship with us. He has set in motion principles for the maximum efficiency and coexistence of His creation to ultimately reflect that community.

Knowing your purpose in life is the ultimate freedom. And it creates true communities where freedom can exist because it is others-directed. It exists for the common good *only* in communion with each other. There is no common good without a community. It's like love. It has no definition until it is given away. It's not love if it is self-contained.

I think you get the picture.

Knowing your purpose in life is the ultimate freedom.

The internet "community" is filled with voices telling us every day that we do not have a purpose other than to fulfill ourselves. If you feel that serving the greater good is about you, think again. It's never about you; it's beyond you. If it's only about you, then it is not true community. And if it's not true community, you'll never have the roots to sustain the tsunamis that will come against us. Like those redwood trees, it takes time to grow those roots so we can become the people we were meant to be.

Take the first step toward unfriending the virtual shortcuts to community. Give your roots time to grow deep, then intermingle with others who will help you stand during difficult times. Leave the "unfriendly" confines of the internet to find your strength in relationship with others. And experience the joy of community that only comes with communion with others.

3

Fleshed Out

THE MODEL OF COMMUNITY

Everyone wants to be part of some community. There is an undisputed internal need to have others in our lives, preferably those who will provide us with one thing we all strive for—love.

But have you ever stopped to ask why we have this need? Where did that awareness of community come from? Does something this deep in our souls come about through a capricious turn of events over time? Or is there a grander design to it that makes us more fully human? Can design happen without a designer? These existential questions have been the subject of debates for centuries by those who hold differing views of creation and anthropology. Often the discussion falls into the realm of either religion or science.

Or maybe it's simpler than all that.

The opening verse of John's Gospel states, "In the beginning was the Word, and the Word was with God, and the Word was God." The Darby Translation goes on to say, "And the Word became flesh, and dwelt among us" (v. 14). So what was the Word *before* that?

As I said, this rather deep theological discussion has been going on for ages. In the traditional Christian sense, we acknowledge that Jesus came to be the payment for humanity's sin so fellowship with God could be restored. Got that. But I tend to take the deep things with my limited human mind and understanding and try to find a common intersection with anyone and everyone, regardless of the position they hold.

I'd like to suggest that Jesus' appearance on the scene exhibited another glorious by-product of God's heart for humankind—to model the original community embodied in the Trinity, and what people could expect that community to look like when divinity is fleshed out. Jesus gave us a sneak peek of what heaven on earth would look like in His prayer in Matthew 6. We all know it as the "Our Father" or the Lord's Prayer. It starts off simply enough: "Our Father which art in heaven" (v. 9 KJV). Then it takes off from there to reveal something truly profound.

This simple prayer gives us a glimpse of the heavenly modus operandi for enjoying a quality of life here on earth. Jesus meant to have us look outside ourselves and beyond our circumstances to God's heavenly kingdom as the focal point for understanding earthly existence. What a mystery, and an opportunity, that we can experience that same kind of relationship now on earth as in heaven (v. 10).

Stop and think about that for a minute.

In effect, earth becomes the temporal training ground for the eternal. And Jesus came to model what true community would look like. He demonstrated that community does not work without communion—others intersecting with each other in loving, giving, sacrificial relationships. The Word became flesh in order that it would be fleshed out. It must be unpacked to be evident, and then be shared. Most often, people find out what they actually have in common *only* by shared experiences. They are not planned or coordinated. They are spontaneous and serendipitous. We find out we like someone because we have intersected with them in some way and who they are is revealed in the context of interaction and personal struggle, work, and play.

Strip away the opportunity to intersect, and you have less of how the universe operates. God revealed that to us by eternity stepping into time. There is no greater revelation of the need for community than this one mysterious act of unfathomable love. And mystery.

Hold that thought. And now, look at what we have today.

We have become such a social-media-conscious world that we now even begin to think in terms of behavioral patterns consistent with social media norms. When people think or act in a manner that we disapprove of, we simply "unfriend" them in the blink of a cursor. We can easily dismiss someone when we remain separated by a firewall of emotional detachment. That's harder to do when we have a relationship that must confront life daily and deal with differences, difficult behavior, and emotional pain. Hard to unfriend someone face-to-face without feeling the emotion behind it.

If we simply "unfriend" someone when struggle inevitably

occurs, we never learn this important lesson: The struggle between two people is often the determining factor in bringing them together, not separating them.

The struggle between two people is often the determining factor in bringing them together, not separating them.

Opting out of a marriage is a tangible example of what has happened in our cultural drift toward the internet's model of instant emotional detachment. We can unfriend a marriage as easily as we unfriend an individual in an online relationship. Unfortunately, statistics continue to reveal that those who go through a struggle in their marriage often end up better off by staying together rather than by splitting up.

Sadly, relationships have become less relational. *We see that played out daily among our children, who seem to have more of a relationship with a cell phone than with another human.*

Emotional detachment does not make for establishing good community, a necessary part of our DNA, as we are hardwired in our souls to need each other. We find that from the beginning of time. When God created humans, He formed Adam and understood that it was not good for him to be alone, simply because to properly and fully express the image of God, more than one being was necessary. So Eve came into the picture to complete Adam. And to complete the image of God.

So the concept of community was born in eternity past and then translated to earth. Humans were made in God's image, which included the image of community. That's why we function best when we have people in our lives who help us understand the world—and help us interpret ourselves to the world.

Jesus was trying to show us that God wanted communion so much with His creation that He was willing to step outside Himself to achieve that. In a sense, to model that, we must similarly step outside ourselves to find community as well.

What does the word community *mean to you? How can you unfriend yourself from the grip of social-media anonymity and begin to speak a common language rather than the foreign language of our strictly social-media culture? What are some practical ways in which you can unpack yourself to another person and flesh out the real meaning of community?*

4

Shared Life

THE CHARACTER OF COMMUNITY

The word *community* has become one of those words people use indiscriminately to describe anything and everything with a subset. This is an amorphous and often ethereal allusion to an audience they want to define for their own purposes, not real community.

Often, people will set themselves up as a spokesperson for this "community" to the point where, if the truth be told, it's really set up as a straw man to further one's agenda rather than actually describing an existing group of people or their actual opinion. Instead, let me offer a description of what a real community looks like—and acts like.

Inherent to the word *community* is another word: *communion*. The Latin transliteration of that is to share something in common, or to establish a commonality with another. Whenever

Unfriended

we think of community, we think of a group that comes together for a similar cause or shares something in common that brings them together.

So what might a true community look like?

Well, I believe that one of the greatest examples of what a community looks and feels like is found in John's Gospel. If you really want a living, breathing example of true community, then Jesus' words as He addresses His disciples before the crucifixion may be one such an example. He begins by giving us an interesting perspective. Although community to most of us implies many, Jesus boils it down to community best defined as one. Not many. Listen to His words: "All I have is yours, and all you have is mine. . . . Holy Father, protect them by the power of your name, the name you gave me, so that they may be one as we are one" (John 17:10–11).

Jesus has built this amazing community of disciples over three years. He could have asked anything from His Father on their behalf, yet He asks only that they be one. There is something powerful about many becoming one.

Now where have you heard that statement before?

As mentioned earlier, if you look on the back of U.S. currency and coins, you'll find the Latin motto for our country, *E pluribus unum*, or "one from many." The strength of the United States of America has always been one from many. It has succeeded because it followed a principle born in the heavens, where true community started in the form of the Trinity. In the language of heaven, one is not singular. One is plural.

In the language of heaven, one is not singular. One is plural.

18

Do you think there is any coincidence that Jesus asks the thing that will truly make this ragtag group of fishermen, tax collectors, and sinners into a true community of believers, that they become one? He continues with another amazing statement: "My prayer is not for them alone. I pray also for those who will believe in me through their message, that *all* of them may be one" (v. 20, emphasis mine).

So Jesus is praying for the extension of this community throughout the age. Another aspect of community, then, is longevity. Community is designed to live beyond itself. It's not about just me; it's about me and everyone after me. Community must have some long-range vision for continuity.

Two chapters earlier, in John 15, Jesus is talking to His disciples about another aspect of true community:

> "As the Father has loved me, so I have loved you. Now remain in my love. If you obey my commands, you will remain in my love, just as I have obeyed my Father's commands and remain in his love. I have told you this so that my joy may be in you and that your joy may be complete. My command is this: Love each other as I have loved you. Greater love has no one that this: to lay down one's life for one's friends." (vv. 9–13)

In these passages, Jesus is laying down the benchmark of not only what His community of believers would look like, but what a true community would look like as well. The two things that would be evident in the character of a community are love and joy. Two of the very things we find sorely missing from much of the social-media interaction of our day.

Sorry, I just don't see a lot of love and joy being expressed between people who are different. Just the opposite. I see snippiness, racism, belligerence, lack of civility, rancor, and the list goes on. If these character traits are missing, is it really an online community—or is it just a mob?

And then Jesus finalizes this passage by saying this: "I no longer call you servants, because a servant does not know his master's business. Instead, I have called you friends. ... This is my command: Love each other" (vv. 15, 17).

So according to Jesus, a true community is best characterized by people who model oneness, love, joy, and friendship among themselves—a caring, other-centered, time-lasting, love-expressing group of people who would die for one another.

Now that's a community anyone would opt in to be a part of.

What community are you a part of that reflects these character traits? If you're focused on being part of an online community only, where you are at arm's length from everyone and the only thing you may be one about is your political persuasion or product-driven engagement, then you might want to "unfriend" all that and become part of the heavenly community that Jesus describes.

5

The Embedded Life

THE INTERSECTION OF COMMUNITY

In recent memory, one of the journalistic hallmarks of the Gulf War was the embedded journalist. We heard and saw war first-hand as it happened. Nothing like being involved and on-site to best understand what people experience.

It's the same thing in life. Being embedded is more accurate than speaking from a distance or from the sideline. Intersection helps us in our dissection of experiences.

I learned that lesson very well after my graduation from Boston University, when I returned home to North Jersey to begin my career in journalism. As part of a desire to further my education, I enrolled in a rather unique program offered through New York Seminary called the Urban Theological Year, taught by noted urban church planter Dr. Bill Iverson. The emphasis of the course was to prepare people for understanding urban street mentality in order to best interpret it.

Coming from my rather comfortable middle-class Italian family model, this would certainly be something outside my life experience. As a journalist and as a Christian, I felt it would offer me a perspective on life that would serve me well as an interpreter of the social sphere—something I knew very little about.

That year, we explored many topics totally foreign to my worldview, like black liberation theology and the politics of poverty, among others. Really interesting discussion among our ethnically and racially diverse group of recent college grads that Dr. Iverson had assembled from around the country who met in his home in Orange, New Jersey. We were a ragtag bunch. White. Black. Asian. Chicano. Southern rednecks. Ex-hippies. It took almost six months for us just to break down the walls between us! But it was worth it. In the end, it was one of the greatest learning experiences of my life.

The first lesson I learned was that getting outside yourself is the foundation of true learning. I often like to say that one cannot look inward to find those things that can only be found outside us.

One particular assignment was really outside the box for me, as well as the rest of the team. Each of us were assigned to live in a rescue mission in Manhattan for one weekend. We would experience what others who entered a mission on a Friday night experienced, and we would not tell anyone who we were, not even the director or staff at the mission. Our objective was simply to observe, interact with the fellow indigents with whom we lived, and then report back to the group the following week as to our observations.

Okay. I could do that.

In order to look somewhat indigent myself, I didn't shave for a week, found the oldest clothes I had to wear, and went into Manhattan early that Friday to walk around in the rain to smell somewhat musty before heading to the mission. When I got to the mission, I stood in line with all the others waiting for a hot meal and a roof over their heads for the weekend. And that's when the lesson of being embedded began.

As I stood there, I got into a conversation with an out-of-town man who decided to engage a prostitute in his car overnight in a no-parking zone. The police discovered them and impounded his car, and it would cost him $300 to retrieve it from the pound. Well, he had no money left after paying a fine for his indiscretion, so he could not get the car and return home. So there he was at the mission. It became plainly obvious that he didn't know how he was going to come up with $300, which was a lot of money in 1973.

That conversation was really quite foreign to me. I asked him why he didn't just call someone in his family to help him out. Or, if that was too embarrassing, go find a temporary job doing anything to make the money.

And then I learned an important truth about the mind-set of poverty. It's one thing to be poor; it's another thing to be poor *and* hopeless. People who have lost hope have lost way more than the ability to look for a job. They have lost the ability to believe that anyone would hire them. Worse yet, the accompanying feeling is that no cares either. The real issue is not finding a job; it's recovering the meaning to life that enables someone to believe that work is valuable to one's identity and self-esteem. The two work hand in hand to forge character.

We see the politics of poverty all around us. Politicians all say they want to create jobs, without knowing or caring to know that providing a job is only good if you provide hope as well. Poverty of the pocket is one side of the coin. Poverty of the spirit is the other. It's not about providing jobs. It's about providing hope. When both needs are met, a person has a much better chance of breaking cycles and strongholds.

As I stood there talking to that man, that poverty of spirit had assigned him to a caste system, and he believed he was unable to break out of the system.

My next lesson came a few hours later after the evening meal. My mother was a great Italian cook. On her very worst day, I never in my life tasted anything like I had that night. I still don't know what it was. Then after the meal, everyone had to take a shower. Our clothes were taken and hung in a room to fumigate them because you never knew where any of these people might have been while sleeping on the streets and this process would remove lice. Everyone was given what seemed like a hospital gown to wear for the rest of the evening and to bed.

But the most important lesson was soon to come.

There was a man playing chess by himself, and I enjoyed the game, so I asked him if I could play. There was nothing else to do. It was not like there were flat-screen TVs with unlimited channels of entertainment. He nodded, and I joined him. And for two hours we played chess. Not a word was exchanged between us. I usually can strike up a conversation with anyone. Not this time.

There I learned the sense of anonymity that poverty of the spirit breeds. And anonymity leads to invisibility. That man felt invisible. With no identity and no hope, he was a ghost to anyone around him.

That weekend in the mission did more to help me understand the politics of poverty than anything I have ever done, read, or heard since. Walking a mile in those shoes opened my eyes to how people should be treated (and why there are no easy answers to anyone's problems without involvement). It also revealed to me that until I actually intersect with people in *that* situation, my understanding is simply lacking. Reminds me of all those who like to say what people need when they have never experienced how they feel. All that does is spread misinformation and fuel our hubris, tricking us into thinking that we've contributed something positive to the national narrative on this topic.

Trying to understand the world through social media without intersection is nothing but misinformed opinion. It allows me to speak from a vacuum of thought, to say whatever I choose without any repercussion. And boy, so many have so much to say about things they know nothing about.

Trying to understand the world through social media without intersection is nothing but misinformed opinion.

As I often say, people like to speak with authority out of ignorance. That's why I look to Jesus as my model for intersection, which gives an expression to the face of humanity. When He walked the earth, He allowed people to touch the hem of His garment, He went to the home of someone whose daughter just died, and He went to a tomb to cry over a friend's death. Still today, He restores hope to those who feel unloved and uncared for. And above all else, Jesus leads everyone to the cross, which is the greatest level playing field of all time. And He dies for us. It's hard to feel unloved and uncared for when someone goes to that length to show His love.

Now that is the ultimate form of intersection that cannot be achieved by a Facebook post or a tweet—or anything written in a blog.

Make an effort to unfriend the tendency to misinform by a lack of involvement. Your intersection in the lives of those around you can be the encouragement they need to break free from their poverty of the spirit and their culture of anonymity. Consider embedding yourself in an environment totally foreign to your worldview. God refuels us not to stay in the garage but to become His vehicles of change.

6

Enriching Agents

THE SALT AND LIGHT OF COMMUNITY

When I was a kid, I lived with my parents, brother, and paternal grandparents in a small North Jersey town not far from New York City. Being very Italian, we had a very large garden, so every spring a large amount of fertilizer was delivered to help us prepare the soil for planting. It wasn't the kind you get today at Home Depot in bags. No, this fertilizer came in truckloads from the local chicken farm. Chicken droppings were really good as a fertilizer. It had quite an aroma, as you could imagine, but it was effective. No doubt, fertilizer has its place and a significant purpose. Okay, now hold that thought while I introduce another one.

In Matthew 5:13–16, Jesus describes the characteristics of what a community that reflects His character would look like. Interestingly, He compares His followers to salt and light. He tells them plainly, so there can be no misunderstanding:

You are the salt of the earth. But if the salt loses its salt-iness, how can it be made salty again? It is no longer good for anything, except to be thrown out and trampled underfoot. You are the light of the world. A town built on a hill cannot be hidden. Neither do people light a lamp and put it under a bowl. Instead they put it on its stand, and it gives light to everyone in the house. In the same way, let your light shine before others, that they may see your good deeds and glorify your Father in heaven.

What are the distinguishing characteristics of those who would be called Jesus' disciples? They would be like salt, to flavor and act as a preservative to society. And they would be like light, to illu-mine the beauty and presence of God in this world and to dispel the darkness that blinds people to all that is good in the world. In essence, His disciples are supposed to be *in* the world—intersect-ing, involved, sweaty—so that people can sense their presence by the aroma of a good deed, a helping hand, and a smile.

A kind word spoken spontaneously and with sincerity reverberates endlessly in the heart of the one who receives it. This doesn't happen in a virtual environment.

A kind word spoken with sincerity reverberates endlessly in the heart of the one who receives it.

For salt to be effective, it must penetrate. For light to be effective, it must have a source and find darkness to counter its effect of the lack of clarity on life. All this is personal. Not virtual. When you have people involved this way, true community can happen in the way that makes the world better.

Jesus said all this salting and lighting would ultimately point people to God and His goodness, not to us. God's presence in the world is three-dimensional. You can't get that while remaining in the world of two-dimensional internet life.

Now let me get back to the fertilizer analogy. I suggest that many evangelicals have exhibited more traits of the chicken fertilizer from my childhood than those of salt and light! I now add the internet to this list as well. There is a similarity to the two.

You see, fertilizer is to be spread evenly over the land to enrich and nourish the environment so that things can grow and be fruitful. A Christ-follower is more than salt and light in the world because our culture needs more than just *preservation*. It needs *replenishment*.

Fertilizer is useful, even necessary at times, to replenish the land with nutrients so it can be productive. Without fertilizer, the land may not be able to sustain the growth of good plants. Weeds begin to appear, and they seem to grow anywhere and everywhere without the aid of fertilizer. They're prolific and can choke the growth of the good plants. Fertilizer can help control the weeds by creating the right climate for good plants to grow so the weeds don't take over the land. All good.

Now take that same fertilizer and stockpile it somewhere. We knew it was there; we couldn't miss it. After all, if fertilizer is stockpiled too long without being spread throughout the land and used as the enriching agent it's meant to be, it begins to fester, smell, and even attract flies. Instead of contributing to the overall productivity of the soil, it becomes useless. If the fertilizer is not spread out, nothing grows.

It dawned on me that sometimes our churches and the internet resemble fertilizer. Both are meant to be enriching agents. That's the job of fertilizer. Ideally, we should be known by the way we enrich the world by our presence. On the other hand, when church folk stockpile themselves in one area without being the enriching agents they were meant to be, they begin to fester, even smell, if you know what I mean. It's not a pleasant sight or smell when that happens. And if you happen to be downwind of them ...

So it is with the online community of those who would choose to only fertilize their own ideas. Are they preserving the land or creating a toxic environment that poisons the minds of those who come into contact with it?

Ask yourself: Am I acting like fertilizer, personally or online? Am I spreading out to enrich my land—or stockpiling myself in such a way that I have an unpleasant aroma?

Just asking.

You might want to unfriend the unpleasant aroma of a stockpiled community of ideas that are void of salt or light, that contribute to the ongoing darkness of personal involvement and online communication. Spread yourself throughout the land and become not just salt and light, but the enriching agent you were meant to be in community with others.

7

God's Silent Language

THE COMMUNITY IN CREATION

All of us are in search of happiness and the peace that comes with it. We all know clichés like "money can't buy you happiness." And we know that an attitude of thankfulness creates a mind-set that fosters happiness.

Happiness does not necessarily happen by chance, as we can take specific actions in our lives to create it. I read something about happiness by author, TV show host, *Psychology Today* blogger, and corporate trainer Robert Puff, PhD, who's been studying and writing about human achievement for decades. I think he hits the nail on the head about one of the key ways to attain happiness.

He suggests that people "go for a walk for 30 minutes to

an hour, and focus on being present with the outdoors. If, after their walk, they still feel just as despondent, then they should give me another call. The result? In nearly 25 years, I've rarely received the second call."[2]

He continues, "When we identify with the present moment and focus on the beauty that surrounds us, we increase happiness. ... When our minds are still, fully present with the here-and-now, and without the mental commentary, then we experience a peace that surpasses understanding."

Did you hear that? Peace that passes understanding! Now where have you heard that before?

Look at Philippians 4:6–7 in the New Testament. Paul is writing to the church in Philippi from a Roman prison. Yes, Paul is in jail facing certain death, and he writes this: "Be anxious for nothing. But, in everything, with prayer and supplication, let your requests be made known to God. And the peace of God, which passes all understanding, will guard your heart and mind in Christ Jesus" (NASB).

Puff continues, "Go outside and find a place where you're not surrounded by many people. This may be a park, meadow, lake, or beach. Find an object to focus on, such as a flower, tree, bird, or water. For one to ten minutes, draw all of your attention onto what you've chosen to focus on. Listen to it, watch it, just be with it. Resist the urge to analyze it, or create a story about it."

Kudos to you, Dr. Puff, for your insight into one of the great mysteries of life! You've identified the right environment where one can begin to understand how the universe works and how God created us to fit into that model.

I'm going to ask this question to illustrate what the Bible and Dr. Puff tell us: Did you ever wonder why it was called the garden of Eden and not the city of Eden? Why did God choose to plant Adam and Even in a garden and not in a city?

Answer: Because being around God's creation points to God and peace rather than being in an environment stripped of God. God creates nature, and man creates anti-nature. I do not believe that true community can be achieved via social-media interaction simply because it lacks this basic ingredient of God's creation and order.

When I want to find out what nature's best plan is for humans to experience peace and fulfillment, I usually go to Scripture. There are many life principles that can be mined from the riches in that book.

So what principles do I find built around the perfect environment of Eden that enable me to find happiness? Let me illustrate that by telling you a story about my childhood.

I love spring—the time of year when we come out of winter hibernation and colors once again come alive all around us. What a reminder that life has beauty if we only take the time to see it. Smell it. Walk in it.

This past spring also prompted me to think about something I never had considered, which came up during a conversation with friends. We were talking about health, nutrition, and overall spiritual health. Somehow the topic turned to how much I always enjoyed working in a garden. Part of my built-in DNA, I believe, stems from my Italian heritage and the many hours I spent working in the rather large garden we had at home. My grandfather, uncle, father, brother, and I would tend it.

When my grandfather was alive, he would prepare the entire garden—almost ten thousand square feet—by hand with a pitchfork. Of course, he was used to hard work because that's all he ever knew. It seemed that extreme perspiration was part of being Italian, which may explain why I became a journalist. (After my grandfather passed away, my father and uncle decided to get close to the twentieth century and get a rototiller to do all that work. We were basically self-sufficient in the summer, as we grew every fruit and vegetable imaginable.)

I have never felt more content and at peace than sitting in the dirt on a sunny summer day, planting tomatoes, cucumbers, and squash, among others. Like I said, I think Dr. Puff hit the nail on the head with his findings and comments. Being one with nature is very much a biblical principle, for several reasons.

The psalmist declares that the heavens reveal the glory of the Lord (Psalm 19:1). Paul, in Romans, reminds us that God's handiwork is revealed in nature and in the heavens (Romans 1:20). Jesus alludes to God's care and presence in His creation when He asks us to trust and not worry about today, for He clothes the flowers of the field and provides food for the birds (Matthew 6:25–34).

Yes, there is an undeniable link between the God of the universe and the universe itself, just as artists have a spiritual connection with their art and often create art that reflects what's deep down in their souls. Nature is God's silent language to us that reveals much about His character. We see order, beauty, purpose, and breathtaking majesty, as well as force and power and even destruction.

Nature is God's silent language to us that reveals much about His character.

To me, it's evident that nature reveals much about the existence of God. So to remove elements of the creation (clean air, trees, grass, lakes and rivers, and creatures) is to remove those very things that God created to bear witness to Himself. When we surround ourselves with less of God's creation, we remove an aspect of God's presence from our lives. As such, the Christian should be the most ardent of all conservationists.

I've come to believe that the more time we spend inside and less time outside in the midst of God's nature, the more chaos we will experience. This may be most evident in cities, where crime is more prevalent and where there is less peace. Yes, you heard me. I believe that our cities tend to be more chaotic and crime ridden, not because there are more people, but because a vestige of God's presence has been removed from the environment, thereby making it harder to find God. I admit, I'm no social scientist and this line of reasoning may be way off in left field somewhere.

But because the environment has been so stripped of God's presence, we have lost sight of Him and His place in our lives. And if we strip away the things of nature that by design communicate a sense of order, tranquility, and transcendence, then society will gravitate toward the antithesis of those things—disorder, stress, and focus on self, which breeds selfishness. Without a God to embrace, we create our own gods to fill the vacuum in our souls for which we've been hardwired.

I really believe the trend toward urban gardening and the increase in millennials leaving the corporate world in favor of organic farming careers (according to latest stats by the U.S. Department of Agriculture) is fueled by an innate drive for people to experience the peace of God in the midst of urban culture that sucks life from us and from our spirits.

The movement in the eighteenth and nineteenth centuries to build parks in the middle of urban environments—Central Park in New York being the most notable—was a direct correlation to provide people with a glimpse of God and a retreat opportunity for citizens to refuel and relax. And the great architects of these parks and gardens, for the most part, were biblicists.

If you're feeling far from God, unfriend the emptiness of the online creation and take a trip to the country. Be still and focus on God's creation, as Dr. Puff suggests. Better yet, put on some old clothes and go sit in the dirt and plant some tomatoes. Listen to the voice of God in the wind as it whips through the trees. Feel His presence in the warmth of the sun. Pray. Sing a worship song. I bet you'll feel a lot better at the end of the day.

8

Fake News

THE EXPORT OF FAKE COMMUNITY

I happen to believe that one of the greatest careers one can choose is journalism. This comment may be a bit self-serving, as my training happens to be in journalism, which I pursued immediately after graduating from Boston University.

Due to certain providential circumstances beyond my control, I soon found myself as a broadcaster, and that's where my career took me. But I have always felt I had the heart of a journalist and still enjoy writing as an avocation. I have taught journalism and have a deep respect for the classic role of the journalist, which is to interpret the social sphere and, as I define it, "illumine what others cannot see."

Fast-forward to our current cultural fixation on the new term that defines the illegitimate child of classic journalism—"fake news." Popularized to the point of absurdity in the last election, the very idea of fake news has played a key role in the alarmingly growing percentage of Americans who distrust the media to present researched and factual observations and interpretations of the news.

Journalism used to be all about observation and interpretation. Today, it seems to be fraught with titillation and misinformation, playing to a growing addiction to voyeurism, for which the internet has been quite responsible in this unseemly metamorphosis. It has become the preferred sandbox and playground for anyone who chooses to question everything and make statements about anything or anyone without any shred of evidence or corroborating testimony of first-person accounts.

Nowadays, many people consider themselves journalists by virtue of their attempts to interpret their social sphere via their preferred choice of social media, in whatever uncivil language they choose to use. You can say anything you want, as facts seem to be afterthoughts, rather than central, to the process. It's real-time observation with no context, no accountability for what one does, and no desire to be accurate in the presentation.

The journalist's responsibility has always been to state nothing more than the truth. And nothing less than the truth. Anything other than that is not the truth. It's an agenda—a mentality that spawned the fake-news syndrome.

And it seems as if everyone has an agenda today. This online "community" of unrestricted inhibition has allowed people to assume the role of self-appointed online spokespeople for whatever agenda they want to propose. No one needs to be right; they just need a platform. So many have created their own "communities" to allow for this deception. So what can be done to combat this fake-news phenomenon? Can anyone belong to a so-called community simply because they self-identify with one?

To begin with, fake news cannot exist in an environment that believes in the search for truth. One of the greatest examples of fake news in history occurred when religious leaders brought Jesus to Pilate with less-than-accurate accusations and trumped-up charges. Pilate confronted Jesus, the person who claimed to be "the truth" (John 14:6), asking, "What is truth?" (18:38)—the same question we ask today.

You see, fake news is not new. It's always been around, and will always be around, as long as people do not want to face that which is true, obvious, and uncomfortable. It's always more expedient to give life to a lie than to put your ego to death. Jesus came to enable us to face our own death to self. Ironically, He called that freedom.

It's always more expedient to give life to a lie than to put your ego to death.

If we are to find freedom today in the midst of fake news, we cannot hide behind the firewall of impersonality found on the internet. Fake environments must come up with fake news to legitimize their fake community. When we put our faith in that which is not real, the end result is usually not very real either. There is so much fake news online that it's hard to tell the dividing line between the real and surreal, deception from misconception, delusion and illusion. Truth is disappearing quicker than the magician's sleight of hand.

Unfriended

I firmly believe that the antidote to all this is to restore each of us to true community—to relationships that will demand integrity, walk in truthfulness, and challenge inauthenticity. The fake communities on the internet will never accomplish that with people who never demand anything from each other but fodder for more controversy and confusion.

The challenge for each of us is to loosen the grip these communities have on us for more consumption of that which is not real. Jesus came to give us the good news, all the time. He promises us the community of people who will demand more of themselves than others demand of them and strive for that which is true because He was the truth. And "the truth will set you free" to find what is real (John 8:32).

If you are desperately looking to be free from the lies and deceit found online, and it's getting harder and harder to know what to believe, then let me introduce you to someone to believe in. Unfriend the fake news of online community and befriend the person of Jesus. His community is from everlasting to everlasting.

9

A Refugee's Tale

THE TRANSCENDENT COMMUNITY

There has certainly been much discussion, handwringing, soul searching, and name calling on the issue of immigration. Aliens, immigrants, "dreamers," and refugees—however you identify them, one thing remains: everyone has a name ... and a story. We see lots of political grandstanding on this issue by all who pick up placards to plead their causes.

As I see it, the problem is that we continue to address this issue as a political one, which may never resolve it. People will boil it down to what is legal and what is not. Or what is expedient. Or what is "fair," which of course can never be measured because fairness is too subjective. There may not be a more subjective term in our lexicon. Then there are issues about security, administration, costs, humanitarian work, and the list goes on.

The more I think about this issue, the more I have come to

believe that there is something beyond the usual watercooler discussion that's missing in this issue. Is there a greater insight to be realized?

After we strip away the politics and semantics, we are faced with basically human issues. And Scripture has ample wisdom within its pages to address most any issue that deals with the human condition.

First of all, stories of immigrants, dreamers, and refugees are replete throughout the Bible. From Genesis to Revelation, the grand story is really all about immigrants and aliens. Surely we can learn something applicable for today from digging into these stories.

From the very beginning, we have drama:

- Adam and Eve were evicted from their first home, never to return. God put a "No Vacancy" sign at the entrance, and no one has ever stepped foot into that environment since.
- Abraham was told by God to emigrate from his homeland Haran to Canaan, and take everything with him to start a new life. He had no idea where God was going to lead him. Sounds like a refugee to me.
- Abraham's nephew Lot was asked to leave his home and not look back because it had become so wicked.
- Jacob had to leave with his eleven sons and their families to live in Egypt as foreigners and aliens. It took them four hundred years before they were able to leave their refugee camps and become immigrants again in another land that God had prepared for them.
- Joseph was the original "dreamer"—with his own dream coat to boot.

- After Assyria's destruction and dispersion of the ten northern tribes of Israel, only the two southern tribes of Judah were left. And then the Babylonians took Judah a few years later. It took the Jews seventy-five years before they were allowed to return to Jerusalem.

So God understands displaced people. Aliens, immigrants, and dreamers are part of the grander biblical narrative. The notion of displacement is more the standard throughout history, not the norm. So what lessons are to be learned from these stories, if any, that we can apply to today's situations? And where is the community in all this?

In the Old Testament, Leviticus 19:34 instructs Israel on the treatment of aliens. It admonished Jews to treat foreigners fairly and not to forget that they too had been aliens while in Egypt. The first thing that strikes me is that it helps to have lived as an alien to appreciate what aliens go through in a strange land. And how to treat them.

Let's pick this up in the New Testament, which refers to Christ's followers as aliens and strangers whose true and ultimate place of inhabitance is heaven (1 Peter 2:11–12). The more I read about what *alien* and *immigrant* mean in Scripture, I find that it's more of a mentality than a geographically displaced individual. I think that's why Scripture has so much to say about the disenfranchised and uses the metaphor of Christ's followers as foreigners in a strange land.

I really believe that our nation is having so much trouble with these issues today because the further we move away from Scripture and its tenets and principles, the less likely we will embody the ethos contained in its pages. *American society may have been more welcoming of its strangers when it was more welcoming of Scripture.* The more we remove the Bible from the marketplace of ideas, the less we will exemplify what it teaches.

Safety and security are some of the key reasons many people want to return to an isolationist policy. I certainly understand the issues surrounding terrorism today, as sound policy must accompany the political will to fulfill one of the prime roles of government, which is to assure the safety of its people. But can sound policy and humanitarian need come together in wise decision-making? I believe it can, but it will take those not driven by agendas to make it happen. It will happen only when decision makers also see themselves as aliens and immigrants and act from that baseline of thinking.

The bigger the political debate on this issue, the more we need to focus on what I call the "transcendence of immigration." And I find no greater illustration of the transcendence of immigration than in the person of Jesus. Talk about a "dreamer." A child born in a manger in a foreign land brought there by his parents. Sounds much like the dreamers of today. The very notion of God stepping out of eternity into time to live among us is the ultimate immigration story. And Jesus was the ultimate immigrant.

The very notion of God stepping out of eternity into time to live among us is the ultimate immigration story.

Scripture says that Jesus came so all of us could experience the wonder of God's love, which created a new community of people who understood and accepted their roles as aliens in this world, and therefore looked to their God as the one who calmed their fears amid turbulence, political unrest, and dislike of their people group.

Jesus constantly was changing the ground rules about who was our neighbor, how we treat others, how we envision our security, and how to be a good citizen. His entire Sermon on the Mount was a counterintuitive manifesto for this new community of displaced people.

Jesus came to define this new community as one comprised of immigrants and aliens *living in their own land.* Their displacement was of the spirit and not one of geography. To best understand the immigrant mentality, we must identify first as an immigrant. It's a spiritual exercise to transcend the physical world's perspective and grasp a new identity as an alien.

This new community was radical to the core. Jesus empowered women, healed the sick, and welcomed children, giving hope to the weak, the poor, and the enslaved. He focused on the outcasts and the disenfranchised, and attended to the lepers—the unclean citizenry of his day, relegated to their own refugee camps. A leper running among the clean was the terrorist of his day.

The world had never seen or heard of the things He embodied. He taught us a new definition of community—simply that everyone who believed in Him would be known by one thing: their love for one another. Everyone was invited to be a part of this community; there were no distinctions. He helped everyone understand that we are all refugees, aliens, or immigrants somehow. When we understand that, our neighbor begins to look less like the bad guy and more like a brother.

That's what the gospel "looks" like when its adherents act it out in the name of Jesus, which leads me to this point: *The inclusiveness of the gospel best illustrates the exclusiveness of its design.* Everyone is welcome. Because everyone is a refugee. We are all in the same boat on the way to the heavenly shore. That's the inclusiveness of the message. And yet it's exclusive to the people who embrace it.

Today, you might unfriend all the rhetoric of fear, scapegoating, and political wrangling over who's your neighbor. Look into the eyes and heart of Jesus and find your peace there. When you do, you will find your neighbor as well.

10

Spiritual Scrutiny

THE TRANSPARENCY OF COMMUNITY

Sometimes I come across a word I use all the time and realize there's more to its definition than I previously considered. Does that ever happen to you?

The word *transparent* came to mind one day as I was writing this book, and it dawned on me how vital transparency is to realizing true community. The dictionary defines *transparent* as "having thoughts, feelings, and motives that are easily perceived" or being "open to public scrutiny."[3]

Now how many of us like public scrutiny? I'm even wary of private scrutiny, let alone the public kind.

Well, you would think that many people like public scrutiny by the way they post comments, pictures, or videos of themselves on their social-media platforms. And scrutinized they will be!

Many of us seem to use social media for the *very purpose* of being seen and scrutinized. A great way to become overly known is to get people to know more about you than anyone needs to know. One of the biggest lies in our social-media culture is that this platform of unbridled transparency will supposedly free us to be more open and honest in our interpersonal communication. And isn't that what everyone wants? Isn't that healthy?

Maybe. But maybe not.

Scrutiny has become so blatantly an expected outcome of social media that it has encouraged the next step and the other side of that coin—the public castigation of everything we now scrutinize. Scrutiny often comes with the very expensive price tag of humiliation, innuendo, or outright lies. You can scrutinize to the point of a total lack of veracity. And if you no longer need to be truthful, well then there's no need to have any guidelines or lines at all. You can then cross any imaginary line with no repercussion at all.

Social media has blurred the lines of the decency, civility, and respect we should have for one another. We've elevated ugliness to an art form. If I don't like your politics, I say so with no restraint, using any kind of language or comment I choose. If I don't like something, anything—a brand of pizza, whatever—I can say anything about it I choose, and it's okay.

Social media has blurred the lines of the decency, civility, and respect we should have for one another. We've elevated ugliness to an art form.

We now treat each other with as much open disdain as we would treat anything else we don't like. There is no difference. Everyone and everything is a target.

And targets are less likely to mean anything to you if you're separated from them by distance and have no emotional attachment to them. Whomever I don't like or whatever I don't agree with becomes an easy target for my verbal assaults or misinformed opinion. Ultimately, distance creates indifference. And then detachment.

Unfortunately, the outcome of indifference and detachment is an absolute lack of personal accountability.

This brings me to one of my points about the necessity for personal intersection to create a sense of true community. The trend toward being transparent on the Web supposes that we can use this platform to confess our sins, practice our indiscretions, and say anything that is on our minds about others and even ourselves. As a society, we believe that the very distance provided by the internet somehow protects us as we disgorge everything we think or say.

So we see the internet as an ethereal garbage dump, or we become ethereal garbage collectors, stopping along the curbs of YouTube videos, posted thoughts, or tweets to pick up everything left out as online trash. Our social media has also become a sewer into which we now dump our refuse of all that is distasteful, prurient, mean, and ugly.

There is very little of worth to be found in the dump, so the more we play there or in the sewage, the more we become like the trash we discard into those environments. It smells, it stinks, and it's foul. So is it any wonder that we become like that which we create?

Jesus says in Matthew 15:11, "Not what goes into the mouth defiles a man; but what comes out of the mouth, this defiles a man" (NKJV). Likewise, what we take in through our eyes, hide in our hearts, and then release out of our mouths identifies us for who we really are.

Unbridled transparency may seem to be the way to get people to know you. Yes, it may allow one to see more. But not necessarily to understand more. And knowing more without understanding more leads to confusion. And confusion leads to fear. And fear leads to anger. And anger needs to be played out eventually as an emotion, since emotions are meant to be expressed. That's why we have them. They reveal the state of our heart.

This is why it's important for people to intersect in real space and time, not solely through the ether of the internet. When I encounter people, I sense their spirit, their laugh, their smile, and their warmth—the very things that make us human. I see joy, pain, and all that life communicates when I can *be* with someone. If I never intersected with anyone, I'd miss all that.

Intersection also challenges my preconceived notions, my own pettiness, and ultimately helps me understand myself. Community helps me to know *me*, not just the other person. Without intersection, I know myself less. And the less I know about myself, the more inward I tend to become.

Intersection adds to my education. Conversely, if intersection helps me to grow, then the lack of intersection shrivels me up. Narrows me rather than expands me. Deflates me rather than inflates me. The more I remain inward, the less I understand myself and develop the skills necessary to live in this world. And then I lack skills to interpret myself to others when I do eventually intersect.

Part of the unfriendliness we see today in our society is caused, I believe, by the inability of people to have true transparency—to achieve such a state of being that people can see right through them because they have nothing to hide. Friends see right through us and still love us because they have intersected with us. And felt all the human things that connect us.

Many of our internet "friends" are not able to see us at all. They can "like" us without even knowing us. When we weigh in on each other's pages, we are not necessarily liking the person, just the experience. Our "friends" may be anonymous and therefore expendable. And easily unfriended.

True community will not allow that. It helps others to see *into* us rather than *through* us. After all, that's what everyone really wants—and strives for.

Today, unfriend the tendency to be transparent to everyone and accountable to no one. You might spend more time getting to be transparent with someone who can actually share life alongside you. Now that is what community is all about!

11

Forgiveness

THE HEAVENLY EXAMPLE OF COMMUNITY

Our diet of news consumption tells us there's an awful lot of bad going on out there. And anymore, it's hard to tell the difference between the good guys and the bad guys. The lines have been blurred so that what was once considered bad is now good. And vice versa. The template for determining either is now up to you, as standards of absolute truth are no longer blurry; they have simply vanished from the minds of many.

You can find examples of that everywhere online. One of the most glaring examples of blurred vision has to do with finding fault with everything and everyone, only dependent on what standard you hold up as being the benchmark for right and wrong. One thing is for certain: when you read what's on the Web, you won't see a whole lot of forgiveness.

True community, however, will exemplify forgiveness as one

of the resounding traits of its existence, as well as the ability to unify people rather than divide them, which is more of what the internet feeds us. The Web is seen as a form of modern-day trench warfare, as we lob verbal and printed grenades on each page we surf. We have become adept at division, and I'm not talking about math.

Everyone is upset about something. A spirit of unforgiveness has been unleashed in our land, and it's consuming us. The internet fosters this spirit, and we must consider the alternative to extinguish this wildfire of the tongue before it burns our entire land with bitterness. That alternative is true community where unforgiveness can be extinguished and understood for the power it has over us for good.

A spirit of unforgiveness has been unleashed in our land, and it's consuming us.

Starting in John 8:15, Jesus gives us a good picture of why forgiveness is important. And why judgment is not ours to take. Apparently, judgment is so weighty that both Jesus and God the Father must agree. So when you and I judge, we usurp the role relegated solely to the Father and Jesus. That's why our judgment is void of love, as it has nothing of the Spirit of God invested in the pronouncement. Love may question and forgive, but it does not judge. Our social-media landscape, on the other hand, is littered with unforgiveness, judgment, and condemnation.

In Matthew 6, Jesus teaches His disciples a little prayer that may be the most well-known prayer in Western civilization. We all know it as the "Our Father." It starts off simply enough, "Our Father, which art in heaven." Then it takes off from there to reveal something deeply profound.

If you carefully look at what Jesus asked us to pray, this simple prayer was giving us a glimpse of the heavenly modus operandi for enjoying a quality of life here on earth. He meant to have us look outside ourselves and beyond our circumstances to God's heavenly kingdom as the focal point for understanding earthly existence. The mystery, and the opportunity, is that we can experience now on earth the same kind of relationship that is experienced in heaven. They are one and the same.

Stop and think about that for a minute.

Forgiveness is a reflection of the heavenly visage. Forgiveness works because it reflects the heart of God. Jesus came to forgive, not to condemn. The more our society blurs who God is, the more we blur our understanding of who our brother is.

Jesus says that heaven is the frame of reference for earthly living. He then adds several more similarities between the two kingdoms. And here's where it really gets interesting. One is forgiveness. The other is to eschew temptations that emanate from the evil one.

Forgiveness is a central theme because it's integral for entering and enjoying God's kingdom, so it's important to begin that lesson on earth. We practice here and now for the real thing later on. We get a glimpse of it on earth and see it fully in action in heaven because only the forgiven and those who forgave will be there (Matthew 6:14–15). When put into practice, it has power to transform.

The most highly publicized example of that in our modern time is how Nelson Mandela exemplified the power of forgiveness to unite South Africa after he was released from prison and ascended to the highest political platform in the land. For many years, he languished in a South African prison, a victim of that nation's apartheid policy. He was a political prisoner in the truest sense of the word. That experience usually embitters a man to the point of no return. Instead, that prison became the crucible for refining his character to embody the one trait that would define him to the world. And change his country. That one thing was forgiveness.

Few people have embodied the power of that concept in our time as Mandela. And this is why he was so powerful a force for change. He modeled what Jesus taught, especially His little prayer in which heaven is the frame of reference for earthly living (Matthew 6:9–13). Mandela caught a glimpse of that heavenly frame of reference while in prison, which forged his view of the eternal. He came to understand the power of forgiveness to release us from ourselves, as well as from a jail cell, and to help us resist the temptation to exact revenge. Lack of forgiveness only leads one back to self-interest. And self-interest closes the gates to real freedom. Mandela learned that true forgiveness has the power to transform one person—or an entire society.

Mandela's focus was so refined in his imprisonment that he learned to see more clearly. He would not let the temptations of revenge or bitterness cloud his vision for uniting his nation. He used the one tool he knew would best forge this new nation—forgiveness. He wanted to see the kingdom of heaven exemplified in his beloved South Africa. In doing so, Mandela became a microcosm of life in heaven right here on earth when he chose forgiveness over hate and vengeance.

We can choose that path as well. Our world desperately

needs to see forgiveness instead of retribution. For a brief moment, the world saw it in Charleston after the shooting that claimed nine lives at the Emmanuel AME Church in June 2015. Several days after the shooting, with the assailant apprehended, family members and friends lined up to say they forgave the shooter, Dylann Roof. What? Forgiving the shooter? The executioner of the innocents? That testimony stopped us in our tracks. That seemed ... unnatural. Yet somehow, in our hearts, it seemed like the right thing to do.

On the other hand, if we continue to assign blame to all the wrongs of the world—whether on rogue cops, Muslims or some other people group, politicians, or our neighbors—we will never experience peace in our society. Or even peace in ourselves. We can reflect on Mandela's life and find the power of interpreting the heavenly kingdom on earth. If so, then forgiveness will be the hallmark of your life "on earth as it is in heaven" (v. 10). That's something that will only be achieved by personal sacrifice, as we live out lives in community to exhibit that type of power.

Another thing about unforgiveness: it keeps us imprisoned and outside the kingdom and the joys that can be experienced on earth. Self-aggrandizement follows this kind of lifestyle. The more we focus on ourselves, the less we can focus on forgiveness. These two are tied together in some mystical way so that they reinforce the other.

That's why Jesus focuses so strongly on these two elements of how kingdom living can be achieved. There is no resisting of temptation without forgiveness and no forgiveness without resisting the efforts of the evil one, who uses temptations as cataracts of the heavenly vision.

Forgiveness

Are you a microcosm of life in heaven right here on earth? If not, unfriend the temptation to use the internet or any medium to render judgment on others. In what ways have you fostered a spirit of unforgiveness? In its place, let an attitude of forgiveness be the hallmark of your life here on earth ... as it is in heaven. Amen.

12

Hands Held High

THE HALLMARK OF THE HEAVENLY COMMUNITY

I have a day job that keeps me quite busy. I have my own company called Renaissance Communications, which I've had for twenty-six years now. It's an advertising/marketing agency that helps promote many of our faith-based films on radio and represent clients and their programs to radio stations for media placement. It's kept me off the street for all these years after I morphed from my broadcasting career into this new opportunity.

People often ask me what I do, and I sometimes respond with not what my company does in a marketing sense, but what I feel my biblical reference point is on a more personal level. I often describe myself as an Aaron (the brother of Moses) who holds up the hands of the people (my clients) whom God has called to part the Red Sea in front of them. It was physiologically impossible for Moses to hold up his arms from sunrise to sunset during a battle with the Amalekites, which is what God required of him so the army of Israel could wage battle and win. So someone was needed on each side to literally keep his arms held up. That's the way I feel at times. It's my job to help people keep their arms up to enable them to get their work done.

You see, understanding our role in the lives of others goes a long way to seeing miracles happen. There are few miracles to be seen in a culture of self-aggrandizement.

True community has a lot of Aarons in it—people holding up the arms of others so much can be accomplished on behalf of the community as a whole. An online community cannot be there physically to hold up our arms when we need to walk through a Red Sea, tell a mountain to move, or fight one of the many battles we face in life. We may come to a point where we're backed up against an insurmountable obstacle that prevents us from getting to the other side. It's frightening because the enemy—whose desire is to kill us—is on our heels, closing in on us. And they usually show no mercy.

It's at that time that we require someone on either side of us to hold up our arms, to be that person in our life who does what we cannot do for ourselves. The holding up of our arms could be a simple belief in our ability to do a job, conquer a disease, or restore a marriage or a relationship. It may be our best friend or a total stranger who comes to our aid.

We can say the Lord will deliver us and truly believe that. Yet God will use people around us as His instruments to help us do what we are physically, emotionally, or intellectually unable to do. We have all heard the saying that with the right amount of faith, we can move mountains. I like to think that the right kind of faith will more likely move *us* so that the mountain no longer blocks our view of the impossible.

There's another interesting perspective to holding up one's arms. It's a universal sign of surrender. When we do that, we make the statement that whatever we're being called to do is beyond our ability to pull off. And that's the position that God wants us to be in all the time. Parting a sea is not an everyday occurrence that anyone can do. It takes a superhuman, providential effort—and strength beyond our ability to exercise it.

Hands held high is acknowledging to God and the world around us that this opportunity is above us, to the point that we admit we cannot do it in our own power and that we need people to help us do what God has called us to do. It's the posture of heavenly surrender and a hallmark of a heavenly community. All this cannot happen unless we know people sufficiently and are involved in their lives intimately to the point that we'd gladly sacrifice on their behalf.

Unfortunately, much of what I see with online "communities" often would rather hold your arms down or pull them apart than hold them up. Criticism, cynicism, mean-spirited words and pictures, and degrading self-photos all contribute to the denigration of the individual and erosion of true community. Because of the constant degrading spirit on the internet, people are always fighting each other rather than holding up each other's arms.

Jesus calls us to a higher model of human interaction that helps those who are facing Red Sea experiences in their lives. That life of the heavenly community is all about supporting others when they're cornered, spiritually or physically. This is the job description for all who seriously want to be a part of this new community, which is stated clearly in 2 Corinthians 5: "All this is from God, who reconciled himself to us through Christ and gave us the ministry of reconciliation. … We are therefore Christ's ambassadors, as though God were making his appeal through us" (vv. 18, 20).

Yet some people believe their role is to be God's defense attorney rather than His ambassador. I think it's fair to say that God does not need a defense attorney to try to prove His existence with angry rhetoric and a defensive spirit to those who deny Him. The distinction is clear: Ambassadors aren't sent to fix the country they're in; rather, they're sent to represent the country they're from.

Ambassadors aren't sent to fix the country they're in;
rather, they're sent to represent the country they're from.

All of us have to choose if we will be defense attorneys or ambassadors. We have to decide if we want to take up an arm to fight with or hold up an arm to allow the power of God to work through a situation. We can either try to win arguments for God or simply model what a godly life looks like.

When you hold up people's arms to do the jobs God has given them in your community, you can become the instrument to help bring them to safety. And by the way, there is one other mighty important fact to all this: holding up their arms to do the impossible may inevitably save you as well!

Unfriended

Unfriend anything that tells you to let go of someone who needs to be lifted up. The world is full of those who are too selfish to lift up someone else, unable to see clearly that they too will be in peril if they do not help their fellow member of the community. Stop trying to defend God and start being His ambassador for those who have Red Seas in front of them.

13

The Hidden and the Healed

THE DISPARITY OF COMMUNITY

Community has a way of attracting two very different kinds of people with two very different agendas: those who choose to blend in and those who choose to stand out. The hidden and the healed, as I call them.

In popular culture, the internet has become an uncharted destination point for the hidden because you can become part of a worldwide "community" that is really an illusion. This online "community" is all about hiding. The larger the community, the easier it is to blend in, almost to the point of anonymity. You can stay locked up in a room unto yourself, headed on the road to nowhere.

The problem with hiding in this community is that you rarely get to intersect with someone who may be the answer to your need. Especially if you are hurting. Those who seek healing have to come out and find their healer. Healing comes when you seek help outside yourself.

The real problem with a social-media mind-set is that it's not really about being social; it's about being safe. We aren't looking for people unlike us. We want people just like us. So we say what we want and receive responses from those who reinforce what we like, what we believe, what we think. In this community, we can aggregate all the "likes" in the world, but that does not mean that anyone truly likes us. I guess that no longer matters. As a result, we stay safe, secure, and distant in our online communities. And we minimize the risk of meeting those whom life throws our way.

But this is not what community is about. The great thing about true community is that it forces us to intersect with people we normally would never have met otherwise—or with people we would not want to meet in any situation. True community goes beyond what we want or like or the need to feel safe and secure. You see, security is not about being safe. It's about finding our identity. This is why I gravitate to the words of Jesus, who promises to bring me security when I find my identity in Him.

In Matthew 8, we read the story of Jesus healing a leper. It says that the man came to Jesus and knelt before Him. For anyone else during that time, as a Jew, it was anathema to be associated in any way with lepers, let alone touch them. You were ceremonially unclean if you came into contact with a leper. People avoided them at any cost. But Jesus breaks down that barrier to show us that His community included lepers as well.

There's a truth deeper than just a healing in this story: Jesus teaches us to make contact with those the world deems unclean.

They too must be in our community. Unfortunately, both the world and the church have people they declare unclean as well. We're seeing such a rise in anger, conflict, and lack of civility in our society because that's the natural progression of lives untouched by lepers.

Christ calls us to be in the midst of broken people, not safe people. He talks about touching the lives of lepers, the disenfranchised, the poor—those most unlike us but very much like Him. He asks us to live a life of love, but love is only defined when it is given away to the unloved and the unlovely. We cannot stay hidden in the type of community Christ has established.

To be honest, this description of these two kinds of people, the hidden and the healed, is especially appropriate for many within the church as well. Those who are unsure of their relationship with God, and of His love for them, find church an appropriate safe harbor for their anonymity. I can put up a front by spouting my Christian clichés, memorizing Bible verses, and doing all kinds of things that have nothing to do with getting closer to Jesus. I can hide by blending in.

Choosing to hide in the church is a convenient option for many. It's easier to play church than be the church. In this case, the church becomes a substitute for the internet to establish your "hiddenness." Either way, you come up short because neither can help you encounter the healing you may desperately need. You must make yourself known to be known.

Choosing to hide in the church is a convenient option for many. It's easier to play church than be the church.

The healed, on the other hand, are often those who don't look for their healing but find it in being like Jesus to others in some context. There is an inner freedom to knowing you are broken. Imperfection can be a beautiful thing. My friend, actress Shari Rigby, has written a book called *Beautifully Flawed*. For those of you who feel you have to measure up to a certain standard before God accepts you, read Shari's story. I love that word picture she uses, as that's how God sees us—and how we must see each other, and ultimately rejoice in our flawed behavior that can be redeemed by God.

Jesus asks us to relinquish our desire to hide. He invites us to find our healing by throwing ourselves with reckless abandon on the mercy of God. Following Jesus is about a relationship that requires seeing Him in others and being Him to others. You really cannot be Jesus unless you're involved with others. Just as self-contained love is not true love, bringing the words and the life of Jesus can only be legitimized by revealing yourself to others.

True community beckons broken people who have no use for clichés, those who need someone around them to help absorb the blows that have broken them. Broken spirits need to be in the midst of hopeful spirits. The church should be an assembly of the broken who come to be healed, not to hide. Ultimately, true community helps us realize that freedom to be human is found in relationship: first with Jesus and then with others He has healed. Only in the intersection and communion with others can that healing take place. The only caveat is that you have to be involved with others. You can't share life when there is no one around you to share it with. Simply, your identity is found through your humanity.

Social media is very antisocial in that it inhibits the reality of a life that Jesus told us to embrace. We remain hidden behind 280-character Twitter grenades easily tossed into conversations with no concern over possible collateral damage. Or we remain hidden to not expose our own foibles and character flaws. And there's no better way to do that than with smiley faces, emojis, and likes. Anonymity may feel safe, but it's really the one-way street to a dead end in relationships.

I'm afraid that the more we spend time online or in church identifying with a false sense of community, the more we will find ourselves hidden and never healed. So if you are feeling anonymous and using either the internet or the church to stay hidden, Jesus has a word for you: "I have come in order that you might have life—life in all its fullness" (John 10:10 GNT). That's the kind of life I want!

Decide to unfriend the hidden life of anonymity. Get off Facebook and get face-to-face with those who need a touch from Jesus. Our world is desperately looking for close encounters of this kind. When hiding ends, community begins.

14

When Worlds Collide

THE REDEMPTION OF COMMUNITY

Scripture tells the familiar story of the woman caught in the act of adultery (John 8:1–11). Her accusers bring her to Jesus as another opportunity to entrap Him on whether He agrees with what the Jewish law at that time said should happen to women in these cases. I can only imagine the smugness with which they asked Jesus that question.

Now let me take you through a possible scenario of Jesus' intersection with this woman and the men with the stones in their hands who were salivating to become her judge, jury, and executioner. Jesus is in the temple teaching, and these men come in with this woman, ready to exact on her what the law required. Open and shut case … or so they thought.

We often use this story in the context of not being too quick to judge anyone, quoting this verse: "Let any one of you is without sin be the first to throw a stone at her" (v. 7). After her accusers slipped away, Jesus said to the woman, "Go now and leave your life of sin" (v. 11). His words serve as a simple but powerful encounter that transformed her life.

Those words can transform our lives too if we realize what Jesus is saying to us.

Now there's another twist to this story that we often miss, one that introduces a necessary ingredient for what true community looks like: *Community is more about redemption than it ever is about judgment.* Yes, redemption. And redemption happens best, and primarily, with intersection. When I come in contact with another in some context that requires forgiveness, I establish a connection that can change both lives forever. Redemption then has a chance to happen.

I really believe that Jesus' first response is not recorded in Scripture. I think that given His compassion for sinners and dislike for the self-righteous, He felt bad for the woman. I think Jesus could have bent down to speak to her, calmed her fears as He does so often for us when we are in dire straits and afraid of those who would stone us, and maybe even shed a tear for the callousness and hardheartedness of her accusers, who felt their self-righteousness gave them the authority to carry out this sentence.

My good friend Dr. Steve Brown says that righteousness without tears is arrogance. I believe this described the accusers perfectly. On a side note, I believe that the world has seen too much of the church's righteousness, and too few of our tears, in these situations. If we would exchange those stones for tears, people might see God's redemption more clearly.

So then Jesus says something that we have recorded so often

about His response to the men: "Let him without sin cast the first stone." And the men walked away. And so, we always use this as an illustration to not judge people, which is one principle to take away from this.

Yet I think there's another perspective to take away from this encounter. I really believe what happened was this: Jesus revealed to those men in their hearts that *they* were the women, and the *woman* was the one with the stone in her hand!

As such, their only response was to drop their stones and walk away.

So when Jesus asks her what happened to her accusers, she answers that they are gone. No one is left to accuse her. Jesus' response is refreshing: "Neither will I."

But Jesus does not end it there. He has one more thing to add, which, at first glance, sounds a little like judgment. Except it goes beyond judgment. He says, "Go and sin no more." You see, Jesus first calmed her, shed a tear (maybe), rid the environment of accusers, and helped the woman understand that He is not about accusing her either. He is ultimately all about redemption. He first loves on her, rids her of guilt, and then, and only then, asks her to repent—to sin no more.

Often, the church starts with sinning no more without first showing love, shedding tears, leaving behind accusations, and leading people to the cross to show what love really looks like. Anyone who sees and feels *that* love will want to follow Jesus and sin no more. Now, *that* is redemption. And that's why this story is more about redemption than judgment.

Here's the distinction I want to make about the difference between true community and what we find on the internet or in other transactions that do not allow us access to individuals where we can feel their pain. The internet is like the religious leaders with the stones in their hand. That environment breeds accusers. True community, on the other hand, is about redemption. It's that simple. The internet is a proven breeding ground for creating those who would be judge, jury, and executioner. That's easy to do online—harder to do in person.

Lest we think this a stretch, how often do we find verbal stones in our hands when responding to social-media issues we dislike. Just read the comments section of many blogs, posts, and tweets. The self-righteous are all over the internet. Accusers of the innocent. Deceivers extraordinaire. Fake news exists plentifully in a fake community.

There's another problem with the internet, when people now dare to become the judge over another. The reason the Bible says we should not judge is because judgment is solely in the purview of God. So when we feel compelled to judge others, we are assuming something that is not ours to assume. The internet has become the courtroom of public opinion of those who want to usurp the role of God in the lives of others.

It's almost impossible to do this in true community because the very act of intersection—that of direct, personal involvement in someone else's life—where you have access of understanding, compassion, and revelation of that person's character, inhibits the opportunity and desire to walk around with a stone to throw at the first sign of someone you don't like or who thinks differently from you.

It's one thing to engage in verbal trench warfare via the internet—another thing to sense the range of emotions in personal confrontation. A verbal collision may hurt for a moment, but it may also be the catalyst for breaking down walls between people. True community will embrace the fallen and shame the self-righteous into letting go of their stones. True community will shed tears for sinners and the broken rather than accusing them from afar. True community will lead people to the cross, not away from it with their hard hearts. True community will offer redemption, not judgment.

True community will shed tears for sinners and the broken rather than accusing them from afar.

Jesus asks us to drop our stones and look into our hearts to see ourselves more fully. He will not allow us to complain about the unrighteous while we stand in our self- righteousness. He didn't just give Christians a model of what true community looks like; He gave it to the entire world to emulate.

Today, unfriend the spirit of accusation you find rampant on the internet. Drop your stones and walk away from your self-righteousness. Jesus asks you to forgive, to offer redemption to a world dying to hear those words: "Neither do I."

15

The Road Less Traveled

THE SACRIFICE OF COMMUNITY

I n Luke 10, we find one of the most well-known stories in Scripture. It's the story of the good Samaritan. We're always hearing about good Samaritans who help people, sometimes at personal risk. Notice the word *personal*. We'll come back to that.

In the New Living Translation, Jesus describes the Samaritan as "despised" (v. 33). Now if we think about that, it's strange to classify someone who is helpful as despised. Why did He refer to the man that way? Because Jesus was referring to the Samaritan from the eyes of the Jewish culture of His day, which viewed Samaritans as outliers to God. Second-class citizens, or worse, who should be avoided at all costs.

I believe there is a more interesting backstory to this parable that is really not about the Samaritan at all. To me, the greater purpose of the story is to illustrate that we find our identities when we take the time to stop along the roads of life and sacrifice our time, our wealth, and our lives on behalf of the people we find strewn all around us, those who are broken, beaten, and set upon by life's storms. Each of us has an opportunity to be like the Samaritan.

Here's the caveat to all this: Treating our neighbors as ourselves becomes a reality only when we have a neighbor to intersect with. You see, in this parable, Jesus is teaching us not just what constitutes a true neighbor. He's enlarging our vision to help us see that we cannot find the broken who He calls us to help unless we too are traveling that same road. We cannot achieve true community with others if we don't help the broken and beaten people we find along our way.

Treating our neighbors as ourselves becomes a reality only when we have a neighbor to intersect with.

The Samaritan was willing to sacrifice his time, his reputation, and his funds to care for the man. We, like the Samaritan, must also respond to the people we meet who have need of help, then sacrifice something of ourselves to meet the need. There is a connection between the use of our resources on behalf of others and the life that Jesus asks us to embody. We cannot help unless we intersect, and we cannot intersect to share ourselves and our resources unless we are traveling along the same road that others use as well.

The story illustrates that the good neighbor is the one who stops to help. It's also about the sacrifice required *when* you stop. Jesus asks us to invest in those we find broken along the road. These investments may never pay us back. And we may use our resources on people who may never thank us.

Nowhere in that story does it say that once the person was healed, he later communicated with the Samaritan to thank him for his sacrifice. And by the way, our sacrifice is also one of the ego. If we do something based on a desire to be thanked, then it's not about being like Jesus.

There is a way you can tell whether you're serving Jesus the right way. Jesus said that His yoke is easy, and His burden is light (Matthew 11:30). So when we are serving Christ and following His principles, what we take on enables us to be light of heart. If we take on the things that are not of Christ, things we have made up to be holy because we misunderstand the essence of the holy, those things weigh heavy on our hearts and minds. They do not bring peace.

Now everyone is all about finding peace. Jesus showed us how we can do that, even when things are caving in all around us. He simply asks us to sit and listen and observe Him, the one who came to offer us a peace we can't get from the world (John 14:27). This verse also tells us how to find this peace: "Do not let your hearts be troubled and do not be afraid." Jesus' peace calms our hearts and our fears.

This would be another tell-tale sign of His community of believers that can stay calm during a storm, have peace through the trials, and stay focused when the lighted path grows dim. He came to offer a new form of community that would elevate truth and compassion to a new level because He would issue a new command to synthesize the ten given to Moses: "Love God with all your heart with all your soul and with all your mind and with all your strength. ... Love your neighbor as yourself" (Mark 12:30–31).

A community that models what Jesus looks like, and therefore wants us to look like, can't be found on Facebook. Or Instagram. We rarely find the broken there. Only nice pictures of our best moments. Or most entertaining. Or most glamorous. Or whatever. But it's not about encountering the broken along our paths, using our resources to help them, and sacrificing ourselves on their behalf.

Unfriend the desire to travel the safe road and to think of your resources as being solely yours. God may have use of them ... and you. If you're looking to be part of a community, take a walk. And see who shows up. You can't do that online. But be prepared to relinquish time, money, or ego on the person God puts in your path.

16

The Radical Encounter

THE INTERSECTION OF COMMUNITY

C hapter 4 of John's Gospel records an interesting encounter between Jesus and a Samaritan woman He meets at a well. This may seem rather unimportant to us, but knowing the history between Jews and Samaritans will bring an entirely different focus to the story. Verse 9 states that "the woman was surprised, for Jews refuse to have anything to do with Samaritans" (NLT).

A little bit of history will help shed some light on this. Basically, Jews who did not intermarry during their captivity in Babylon, which was God's command to them, felt that those who did intermarry (Samaritans) were unclean and should not be associated with. They were considered half-breeds and not real Jews. No respectable Jew would ever intersect with them, let alone a man speaking to a woman. So Jesus was again committing a real no-no this time.

Often, when Jews had to travel throughout the region, they would purposely take a much longer route and go around Samaria so as to not even step foot in that territory. But Jesus breaks with all custom and teaching by traveling through Samaria, then being at the well to address the woman. She is taken by surprise by this encounter, which is as strange to her as it would have been to a Jew of that day. Just like Jesus, isn't it? He constantly surprises either side of a conflict and fits in neither prescribed box.

Our culture has become notorious for taking sides, thus creating divisions among people and along political party lines, racial lines, ethnic lines—you name it. We seem to now define ourselves into individual subsets of people who think and act alike. And nowhere is that more evident than in our current social-media experience. We create online "communities" of people who are like us: they enjoy all the things we enjoy, think politically like us, raise families like us, and mirror us in many ways. The problem is that we most grow emotionally and intellectually as individuals when we intersect with those who are different from us. And if you really want to learn about life, hang out with people who are radically different from yourself.

When we constantly engage with those who only reinforce our thinking, rather than challenge it, we never learn anything other than what we already believe. Unfortunately, the longer we do that, the more stunted we become in our thought life and our appreciation for the diversity of life all around us. We can only repeat what we already know, and our conversations begin to sound like a scene from *Groundhog Day*.

> Only when we go out of our way to meet people unlike us will the world be surprised and make it a point to tell others about us.

I think that Jesus included this story simply because of the significance of this one thing: only when we go out of our way to meet people unlike us will the world be surprised and make it a point to tell others about us. Unfortunately, we deny ourselves the opportunity to be surprised by our off-course adventures, like Jesus' encounter at the well. Happiness often comes when we least expect it. Remember opening that Cracker Jack box as a kid? Mystery is a great reminder of the adventure of expectation!

When the Samaritan woman awoke that morning, she had no idea she was going to meet the Messiah. And she would not have, had Jesus not purposely decided to intersect with her.

Jesus most exemplified the characteristics of community because He was community embodied in everyday humanity. What He did, where He went, and how He treated the people He encountered—all of these give us a glimpse of what true community looks like.

Each of us can have a "woman at the well" experience. But it will take a desire to establish a connection with someone unlike us or someone we're told is not even interested in us. We must go out of our way to get in front of someone God wants to put in our path. Once we actually do that, I suspect there will be great surprises in store for everyone. Because community is all about the surprise. As Forrest Gump so articulately explained to the lady on the bus stop bench: life is like a box of chocolates; you never know what you'll find until you dig in and bite down.

Looking for a little community beyond the norm? Get offline and get in line to find people who need to intersect with you and hear what you have to say that will change their lives. And change yours. Once you do that, your life will take on new meaning, one you hadn't planned on. Maybe those you intersect with will be so surprised that they cannot help but tell others about what they've just experienced. And maybe you'll have a story to tell as well.

Today, unfriend the desire for your social-media sameness. Let your computer sleep while you step out. Spend some time at the crossroads of life to surprise someone with the gift of your presence. And find true community. You may really enjoy what's in that box of chocolates.

17

The Mary and Martha Syndrome

THE SERVANT COMMUNITY

Like many people, I prefer to learn by hearing or reading stories that help illustrate greater universal truths rather than just memorizing facts. One way I do that is to reflect on familiar biblical stories replete with great truths that can be appreciated by all people. If you dig deep enough, you'll find hidden gems of life principles buried throughout the Bible.

There's always a story behind the story. The venerable broadcaster Paul Harvey called it "the rest of the story." And one of the stories that I believe has greater meaning to a larger picture of how community works best is the story of Jesus walking into the home of Mary and Martha, the sisters of Lazarus, whom Jesus later raised from the dead. Here's the rest of this story.

Martha invites Jesus to come into their home and then spends all her time making food for Him and the disciples, while her sister Mary sits at Jesus' feet and soaks up what He is saying. And doesn't lift a finger to help. At first glance, it seems like Mary is loafing and does not care that Martha is doing all the work. Seems unfair to Martha. Right?

Well, Martha chides Jesus for not telling Mary to help. Surely Jesus sees the inequity here and will do something about it. But Jesus' response is not what Martha expected to hear, which is usually the way He responds to situations. He says, "There is only one thing worth being concerned about. Mary has discovered it, and it will not be taken away from her" (Luke 10:42 NLT).

Now that's clear as mud. Until you start thinking about the rest of the story. Basically, Jesus is helping Martha see what true biblical community looks like—centered around Jesus, being with Him, and listening fervently without distraction.

We are all like one of those two women when it comes to establishing community with Jesus. Like Martha, we invite Jesus in and then get so preoccupied with doing things *for* Him that we miss what He really wants—for us to do things *with* Him. Jesus is telling us that listening may be more important than doing anything because we actually must first hear what He is saying to us in order to do what He asks of us.

Like Martha, we invite Jesus in and then get so preoccupied with doing things for Him that we miss what He really wants— for us to do things with Him.

He goes on to say that Mary's devotion to His presence, and the relationship that ensues, will stay with her always. She will learn something, hear something, and become something because of her desire for that relationship with Jesus that only can happen by sitting still and listening to His words. Just being with Him is all that matters.

Martha failed to realize that when we are so preoccupied doing things for Jesus that we believe He wants, which may be good in and of themselves, we may miss what He has to say that will find its way deep into our soul and stay with us. Just as He has promised never to leave us, so will what He has to say to us never leave us. Knowing someone's heart is the first step to really knowing them. This is what community does. It establishes a link between individuals that can continue forever.

One principle I take from the encounter with Mary and Martha is that we first need to sit at Jesus' feet and listen. Being *with* Him prepares us for the work to come when we do stuff *for* Him. The principle of community exhibited by Mary is this—how we respond to Jesus reflects how we will respond to others.

There is also a broader principle that I draw from this story: we can be so busy doing stuff for the things we worship that we can suffer from the Martha syndrome—being in the presence of someone holy and glorious and entirely missing His impact on us by thinking we have to do something other than simply enjoy Him. We become enslaved to the product of our desires and often forget the person we desire to please. Instead, Jesus invites us to sit and be still and learn how to serve Him.

And by serving Him, we serve each other best.

When we can love our neighbors as ourselves, we have true community. That kind of community spawns a commitment to each other that has staying power. Its members won't forget each other as soon as the storms hit. But to truly exemplify this type of community, we must first remain still and listen at Jesus' feet. That's what Mary was sensing.

Now I do believe that Martha's heart was right. She felt she had to do stuff because Jesus was in the room, which may have been necessary as well. But only when she complained to Jesus that Mary was not helping and asked if He could get her to do so did Jesus respond.

There may be another issue here too—not whether either Martha or Mary were right. It may be that Martha thought that Mary should be doing the thing that Jesus *did not* want her to do, which was stay by His feet and listen and care for Him that way. Wanting others to do what we do—and not respecting what they're supposed to do—is a perspective we often miss. I think Martha missed it. And I think we miss it today with all the busyness that prevents us from sitting and listening to what God has to say to us. True community involves taking time to be with people without an agenda.

Now there are times to do things *for* Jesus. And He modeled that for us when He appeared before the disciples after the resurrection and asked them to go into the world and make disciples.

That was the start of the Christian community—one that communed with each other, intersected with each other, sacrificed for each other, and died for each other.

The Mary and Martha Syndrome

Unfriend anything that lays a guilt trip on you, because that is not the Spirit of Christ. Build time to hear from God in your community. It will be a better place for knowing truth. If you are a Martha, serve gladly and do not ask Jesus to get someone else to do what you do. And if you are Mary, your job may be to teach others about what Jesus is doing. And that can only be done while sitting and listening first.

18

The Bully Pulpit

THE COMMUNITY OF COWARDICE

My TV blared the news of yet another tragic story of a young person who committed suicide after being subjected to online bullying. My heart breaks over the unnecessary death of one so young and the callousness of those who use the Web to tear down rather than build up. It's hard to fathom why someone would choose suicide because of someone else's meanness.

This was totally unheard of when I was young. I keep asking myself what's happened in our culture to drive young people to such a state of hopelessness and despair and pain that death seems like the only way out. As kids, we were always told to watch the people we hung around with. In a strange twist of that saying, the internet may be the worst companion a young person can have. There's a glaring deficiency to the internet that has eluded many people, and that's the deficiency of true community.

The Bully Pulpit

Many people have developed an unrealistic reliance on social media to build a community for themselves and a buffer against the world. This is grossly misunderstood. The online "community" is a fraud—a highly sophisticated *illusion* of community. Our social-media experience has blurred the lines of decency and respect we should have for one another. For example, if I don't like your politics, or anything about you, I can say so with as much foul language or as many disparaging remarks as I like. And if I really don't like another person, I see no difference between venting my feelings about that person as I would about anything else I don't like. We can treat each other with as much disdain as we would some inanimate object that simply doesn't interest us. There is no difference.

Or I can use my social-media cover to bully anyone to make myself feel better, probably because I have as much pain toward myself as I want to inflict upon you. Actually, this kind of behavior is merely another form of self-reflection. Those who engage in online bullying are actually looking inward and acknowledging their own hurt by their action.

The internet has elevated cowardice to a national pastime—with tragic consequences.

Adult bullies are rampant online as well. They use this vehicle to spew their venom of racial slurs, ethnic intolerance, and disdain for everything not like them. They can say all these things with impunity. Sites that cater to this mind-set and celebrate this type of activity and behavior are prolific. The internet has elevated cowardice to a national pastime—with tragic consequences.

There's another pattern that has developed over the years that may explain the power of the internet over our children. I've heard social scientists say that the brains of adolescents are not yet fully developed to handle stress, decisions of a great magnitude, or complicated reasoning. That's why parents, friends, and family are vital to young people as a buffer from forces that assault their hearts and minds, tearing them apart emotionally.

I learned this important lesson some years ago when my daughter was young. My wife had MS and, though very stable, was still challenged in her ability to get around. As a result, I had many other responsibilities around the home, and life can be hard as a caregiver. I had to give up some things I enjoyed doing. Change my life. Sublimate my needs for another's.

Now that's a hard-enough lesson for an adult to embrace. It's even harder for a child to figure out. This came to a head one day when my daughter was around nine years old and began to understand the frustrations caused by her mom's limitations. In a world of soccer moms who seemed to be at the beck and call of their kids, my daughter did not have that same experience many of her friends enjoyed. What seemed normal for everyone else was not the norm in our house.

One day, when another opportunity to do something with her friends was not realized because of her mom's physical limitation, the frustration was just too much for a child's mind and heart to comprehend. I heard her burst into tears and run downstairs to the basement, where she lay crumpled in a corner, repeating, "It's not fair."

As a father, how do you respond to that?

All I could do is just be there, hold her, and do my best to assure her that despite how "unfair" life may seem, I would be there to love her. My role was simply to let my presence somehow absorb her fear and anxiety, which are the real emotions behind what she was feeling. Holding my daughter that day helped me better understand how much God wants to hold us when we go running to hide from the frustrations and fears we encounter in life.

On a side note, the alarming trend of absentee fathers has left a gaping hole in how children process what is happening all around them today. A father's presence helps to absorb the emotion of feelings children cannot process; a father's absence limits that opportunity. Being there is half the battle. The other half is simply silently loving our children. That's what a parent does sometimes. Just be there to help process feelings.

As parents, we want to provide a safe haven for our kids. For most of us, those safe havens have more to do with emotional safety than physical safety. We want to protect our children from the "unfair" treatment they will receive just by going through life, like bullying. We want to be there when they ultimately collapse under the weight of anxiety and fear. We yearn to "take" the pain from them, well aware that we cannot. So the next best thing is to share the pain with them. And the only way to do that is to be there. No app can do that.

The presence of the parent or even a friend at a time like that is unlike anything else in the universe. That's because it mimics what the heavenly Father feels for us, His children, when we need similar comfort.

I elaborate on this incident because it illustrates what I believe to be one of the reasons for the increase in online bullying. One thing we never talk about on the news or read about anywhere is the breakup of the family unit. With the abdication of so many fathers and mothers of their respective roles, children have no one to turn to who can help them absorb these feelings of abandonment and rejection.

When a young person has nowhere to turn, and no one to turn to, that's a problem. When your community is broken or nonexistent, your self-esteem may be as well. On the other hand, activity in a group of people builds identity, which helps to build and mold a community. The intersection with like-minded humans builds your ego and your "wantedness" in life. You feel like you belong.

Strip away the things that build a positive self-image, your feeling of "belonging," and you're left with a hole in your heart and soul that many try to fill from the empty well of online activity. So instead of building true community that requires intersection and communion, you enter into a false world of friendships. When people send mean things to you, those things compound your already negative perception of yourself.

You can run from the internet physically but not emotionally. Therein lies its danger. And there's one more thing. For centuries, we were told we're made in God's image. And that we have value. We have worth. During this past generation, however, the secularists have taken over the narrative, rejecting the notion of a God who's involved in our affairs. They say there's no God, that we're just evolved beings, created for no distinct purpose, and that, basically, we're cosmic accidents.

If you're told you're an accident from an early age, and not a glorious creation made in God's image, that teaching only further contributes to your lack of identity and feelings of worthlessness. That feeling of brokenness is fueled by others who are equally broken and crying out for attention. It's so much easier to tear someone down to make yourself feel better. And there's no better place to do that than within the anonymity of the internet.

Bullying finds that hole you may have dropped through. Maybe you feel trapped, feeding daily on the lies you've been told—simply because you may not have a family or a friend to speak love into your life or buffer you from the misinformation about you that the world offers. Without a true family, you may look for a surrogate family online, one that's not that lovely to be around and only dysfunctional at best. The internet "family" is the wrong crowd to rely on to ascertain your worth.

Unfriend the online "community" of liars and cowards. Turn off the computer and turn on with people who speak your love language. Get in with a community that will share life with you, not suck it from you. You have much to live for.

19

The Currency of Heaven

A COMMUNITY OF TEARS

"You keep track of all my sorrows. You have collected all my tears in your bottle. You have recorded each one in your book" (Psalm 56:8 NLT). I always thought it strange as to why God would save my tears. Some interpret it to mean that God saves our tears as an example of His care and love for us. But I think there's more to it than that. Really, you only save something that has value. So what value would your tears have in God's eyes? And what does that have to do with community?

Well, we cry equally for joy and pain, for laughter and sorrow. Tears reflect how we feel and, at times, are a release valve to allay the pain and suffering we encounter in a world filled with brokenness. They act as a catharsis to cleanse our hearts during grief, and soften the hard ground of cynicism that tends to shut out people from any expressions of love. A flood of tears will often wash away walls we build around ourselves to keep out those with whom God directs us to share life. As such, tears act as a pathway into the life of community. In a real sense, tears are a currency of heaven. That's their value.

In a real sense, tears are a currency of heaven.

This is why I believe Scripture says they are saved and stored. God will use them as investments on our behalf to establish our humanity. And that is something God desires for everyone.

I have come to the conclusion that you can't have true community without establishing an ongoing, intimate connection between yourself and others. To be truly human, you have to feel others' pain, share their laughter, sense their joy, and experience their grief. The intersection of you with others, and all the emotional things that happen when connections are established, is one of the unique traits of being fully human.

Jesus expressed that very well so we could see it in action when He made His way to the house of His friend Lazarus and then to the tomb. John 11 records that story. And it also records that Jesus wept—one of the few times in the Bible that tells us that Jesus cried.

Interesting that it would be for a friend who died, and not for the many other circumstances He often found himself in. He didn't cry over people's lack of theological knowledge, Roman intrusion, government ineptness, the devil's lures, or a host of other things; rather, He wept over the loss of a friend. He then wept again as He looked over Jerusalem, bemoaning their hard-heartedness: "If you, even you, had only known on this day what would bring you peace—but now it is hidden from your eyes" (Luke 19:41).

During the same scene, Jesus also says, "How often would I have gathered your children together as a hen gathers her brood under her wings, and you were not willing!" (Matthew 23:37). He knew that this rejection would deny many people the peace they so badly needed and the joy they would have experienced by recognizing Him and what He could offer.

Jesus wept as a way to express His humanity. He understood that intersection with another individual in the context of sharing life together is one of the most human things you can do. Humanity is best exhibited as we share life with others—sharing experiences, sharing meals, and ultimately sharing ourselves. I cannot give myself to others unless they can look into my eyes, listen to my voice, hear my heart, hold my hand, and experience my joy and pain. And vice versa.

One of the great downsides of trying to achieve community online is that I rarely can get to the point in a relationship that realizes the emotional and spiritual attachment as described above. I am more prone to shed tears over someone when I have established an intimacy with them. That's the essence of love. The connection we establish with others so we feel with them, believe in them, sacrifice for them, and share dreams and visions of them. The degree to which we establish these kinds of connections with others is commensurate with the love we have for them. We cry more easily when we are running on all these cylinders.

That's why God saves these tears. They are evidences of how we have understood His command to love one another and share our lives together. How we have understood clearly that all are made in His image, and that He loves all people. It is our responsibility to act as His representatives on this earth. And one of the outward expressions of being His representative is how we shed tears for others because we have accurately modeled His love for mankind.

Our tears testify to God's heart for His creation through us.

I firmly believe that our humanity is not primarily social; it's spiritual. And one of the greatest barometers of that spiritual life is our ability to weep. It goes beyond what is seen to what is felt. Simply, I believe tears are also the emotional language of the soul. Our weeping brings heavenly dividends that increase through our shedding of more tears. They are bankable in the economy of the kingdom of God.

To achieve the true humanity you seek, unfriend the lie of long-distance community that elevates detachment from others as a viable way to establish relationships. It can't happen to the extent that Jesus asks of us for our involvement in the lives of others. And He said that the things we do for the least of these, we do them unto Him.

20

Puppy Love

THE COMMUNITY OF GOD'S CREATION

I lost a friend not too long ago. Mocha, our thirteen-year-old Shih Tzu, succumbed to old age and illness. We received the call from the pet hospital at 2:30 a.m. the day she died. Despite the heroic efforts they undertook to save this gentle creature, the complications were just too much for her little heart.

Mocha was the cutest, sweetest little dog one could ever hope to have. She was a therapy dog for my wife through her illness, an oasis of love and peace who allowed my daughter to relax and forget about the daily rat race of working in Manhattan.

Romans 1:20 clearly states that God's revelation is displayed in nature. You just have to look at creation and see something beyond anything we can even envision: the majesty of mountaintops against a blue sky, the infinite and expanding expanse of space that seems to have no end, the beauty of a sunset, the marvel of wildflowers that seem painted on valley floors.

To me, this little creature was as majestic, marvelous, and beautiful as everything else in God's creation. And a dog's unconditional love is available to anyone, like the beauty of the sunset, the mountain majesty, and the wildflowers. You just need to choose to look.

As I reflected on this, it dawned on me how representative of God's character Mocha was in this regard. The fact is that God's presence is not just seen in nature but in His creatures as well. Mocha's daily display of tail-wagging joy brought light into the home. I swear I even saw her smile a few times.

The fun thing about Mocha was that whatever the disagreement in our household between us humans, she was always on everyone's side. She would always agree with me. And she'd always agree with my wife. Or my daughter. To Mocha, it didn't matter who was right. Because being right was never the issue. Just being was the issue. And loving.

During many a tense family argument or situation, I could always turn to Mocha and ask her what she thought. "Mocha," I'd say, "who's right, me or Mom?" And the very thought of asking a dog her opinion broke the ice, melted tensions between us, and restored peace. We could laugh again, when a moment before we could only scream or try to get our points across.

Research has shown without a doubt that people who have dogs are happier, have lower blood pressure, and seem to enjoy life more. Of course. That's the purpose of a dog—to help us enjoy the life that God gave us and testify to His presence. Unfortunately, we're often too busy to take time to realize it. We fail to see that a dog is God stepping into our life in the form of the creature He designed to love us unconditionally.

Our Mocha was a living, breathing expression of the Creator, who came in the form of this harmless being to show us that love and humility is powerful and life changing. In the same way, He came to earth in the form of a child in a manger to confound the wise and the proud. The complexity of God's simplicity still overwhelms me.

The complexity of God's simplicity still overwhelms me.

This is what dogs do. They still our hearts, express love to even the underserving, and slow us down to hear the voice of God among the dissonance life throws at us. And that was our precious little Mocha, who inspired me in her death as she did in her life, helping me see what the world needs: a lot more dying to ourselves and a lot less holding on to what we want.

Somehow, Mocha's life made me think about our current political climate these last few years, with all the rancor, tenseness, and vitriol on every side. So I challenge members of Congress to have a dog at every session, particularly the ones where they tear into each other, say mean things about each other, and allow hubris to rule, rather than humility and self-deprecation that would best serve the people who put them there. Dogs don't have aisles. They just have love. So what if Congress no longer had aisles but only love? What if they really had a community?

Really, we are told that you cannot be mean when laughing and smiling, as that's what the dog would help you with. This would be a cool thing to see on C-SPAN. Even though any dog would do, I'm partial to Shih Tzus because they are so small and cute and nonthreatening. And regardless of what you say to them, they just wag their tails in appreciation and follow you wherever you go.

God's creation expresses itself in many ways. But it can't come virtually. The reality of allowing an animal's love to infect our lives and become a part of the family can only be experienced in real time with God's kingdom. Intersecting with Mocha for thirteen years enriched our human experience.

So that's my story. Mocha taught me much. I bet many of you who are reading this have dogs just like Mocha. If you have not done it lately, really take a moment and focus on your dog's face. You may just see a smile.

Today, unfriend the lonely existence of just dealing with humans. Don't just interact with people online as your primary way of experiencing life. Let another member of God's creation give you a perspective that cannot come from another person. Round out your life with a pet and see how more human you become.

21

Sacrifice

THE COMMUNITY OF THE CROSS

One of the criminals who hung there hurled insults at
him: "Aren't you the Messiah? Save yourself and us!" But
the other criminal rebuked him. ... Then he said, "Jesus, remember me when you come into your kingdom."
Jesus answered him, "Truly I tell you, today you will be
with me in paradise." (Luke 23:39–40, 42–43)

would think that most people are aware of Jesus' death on a
cross. That event has been the subject of a number of movies,
books, and media images, ad infinitum. To some, it's a simple
historical event with no bearing on their life today. For others,
it is a reverent symbol of their faith. And to many, it's a good
design for a piece of jewelry.

But I would like to suggest something a bit more radical—that

Jesus and the two men on either side of Him on Calvary repre-sent one of the most definitive and extraordinary examples of community you will ever hear of.

This story of Jesus and the two criminals illuminates a greater truth we may never have considered: sacrifice is an essential part of community. And the understanding of the sacrifice made by Jesus to establish that community is nowhere better illustrated than by the responses of the two criminals—symbolic of you and me. One wanted relief from his situation; the other wanted to be present with Jesus despite the situation.

We can be like the one man who mocked Jesus and won-dered why He did not just save Himself. I suspect that's what most of us would say. That person could only look selfishly for deliverance. Or we can be like the other man, who responded differently. He looked at the situation, honestly confronted him-self with the truth in the hour of his need, confessed who Jesus was, and looked to Jesus to remember him when He got to His community. His eyes were on who Jesus was; the other man's were on what Jesus might do for him.

The second man's theology is not what saved him. It was, instead, his revelation of who Jesus was and his desire to be part of the kingdom of God. That is the kind of community that Christ asks us ultimately to be a part of: the heavenly one.

The story also tells me this: *We've always identified how much it takes to receive Christ, but no one has ever determined how little it takes.* The thief found that out. On the cross, Jesus provided us a perspective of what happens when He invites us to become a part of His community.

First, He leads us to the cross in order to die with Him. We have one of two choices—mock Him or accept Him. We all must go there at some point in our lives to answer that question. If we seek to hang alongside Jesus, we have only two choices. We can believe or disbelieve. We can see ourselves in Jesus, or we can see us apart from Him. We can ask Him to save us from our situation, or we can ask Him to save us. Period.

Jesus made something else very clear: *There is no redemption or entry into the heavenly community without sacrifice.*

You and I are Jesus' representatives to model the heavenly community on earth, as it is in heaven. Our community life on earth is simply a microcosm of the heavenly community, which is to reflect all that Jesus was and is. And that means we are to make sacrifices on behalf of others who hang with us as well. A third entity was necessary on Calvary to make that community attainable, and that was the sacrificial lamb (as Scripture says in Leviticus 4–6) that could atone for the people on either side.

Second, Jesus' community also requires giving up something for the greater good. There is an element of substitution in that equation. In other words, I exchange something I have with another for that someone's benefit. Without an exchange or a substitution, there is no sacrifice. Jesus wanted us to see that on the cross as well. He exchanged places with the criminal who believed in Him so He could taste death and the criminal could have life.

The greatest mystery of all in the Christian faith is why and how God could care enough to substitute a part of Himself on our behalf. It doesn't make sense. But love rarely does. Love of my children or my spouse would dictate that I would gladly substitute myself for them, if necessary. Why do soldiers substitute themselves in death for a country's right to live?

Might the answer be that substitution is woven into the very fabric of the universe, once more reflecting the Creator of that universe? It's part of our DNA because it's part of the way God set this world in motion. And Jesus modeled the most glaring extreme example of substitution on that cross at Calvary.

Another thing about substitution—it can never be done vicariously. Or virtually. True community enables us to sense the sacrifice, the anguish, and the realization that someone cared enough for us to assume that third position on that hill. All of this must happen in the context of being with others.

Third, with sacrifice comes redemption. And restoration. Jesus promises to fill us with His power and love, to the point of overflowing. Yet Scripture says we are all broken clay pots in need of that redemption. Did you ever try to fill a broken or cracked pot with water? Can't do it. The liquid leaks out before it reaches the top. When we tap into the community of the cross, despite our brokenness and cracks, we can be filled to overflowing with God's presence. That's the word picture we're given.

And finally, that heavenly community is also a community of forgiveness. That can't be done other than in person either. Forgiveness frees us emotionally to let go of that which holds us back from being fully human. Jesus was clear in His Sermon on the Mount that only the forgiven and those who forgive would join Him in the heavenly kingdom. God's capacity to forgive exceeds our capacity to sin beyond His forgiveness. Jesus plainly tells us that.

God's capacity to forgive exceeds our capacity to sin beyond His forgiveness.

The wonderful news is that everyone is invited into this community of believers; unfortunately, not everyone accepts the invitation. Some people refuse to believe that God can accept them for who they are or what they have done. But He does. Now that's definitely good news! That's the kind of community I want to be a part of.

Today, unfriend the thinking that you can have all that Jesus wants of you apart from sacrificing yourself on behalf of others. The community of the cross will require you to only want to be with Jesus, regardless of your situation. He's not there to remove you from your hardship; His community exists to help you through the hardship.

22

Families, Communities, and Societies

THE COMMUNITY OF SCIENCE

By Michael Guillen, PhD

I will never forget that fateful day.

After having been born and reared in Los Angeles, after having graduated from UCLA, I boarded an airplane at LAX and said goodbye to everything familiar to me: my family, my friends, and my faith. I was headed to Ithaca, New York, to earn an MS and a PhD in physics, mathematics, and astronomy at Cornell University—about as far away from home as I could possibly get and still be in the United States.

Unfriended

When I arrived, I was greeted by a physics professor—I won't disclose his name—who was less than warm and welcoming. He ridiculed my feelings of homesickness, offering no compassion whatsoever. (Years later, I discovered he was a very unhappy man, and we became friends.) For the first time in my young life, I truly cherished something I'd always had and yet taken for granted: family. Mine happened to be a tight-knit, Hispanic, nuclear family, but healthy families of all descriptions offer the selfsame benefits: love, loyalty, and self-sacrifice.

That last precious quality—*altruism*—is what social scientists see at the heart of communal relationships. Those tight, selfless bonds commonly exist between people who truly love one another, such as family members and best friends. By contrast, reciprocity is at the heart of so-called exchange relationships, the other major category of human associations. These are bonds that commonly exist between coworkers, acquaintances, and strangers.

In communal relationships, people do things for one another without expecting payback. In fact, if you're on the receiving end of an unsolicited communal kindness, paying it back is not a good thing. It diminishes the potency of the loving gesture and downgrades the relationship from communal to exchange.

In exchange relationships, people do things for one another, expecting something in return. If a coworker pays for your lunch one day, you better reciprocate the kindness, and soon, or you'll be in trouble. In an exchange relationship, it's nearly always tit for tat.

In today's age of social media, it is more important than ever that we grasp the profound difference between these two major kinds of relationships. Only then can we fully appreciate social media's assault on our families, communities, and societies.

Real-life families, as I've already indicated, are typically held together by communal relationships. Mom and Dad sacrifice endlessly for their children out of a love that is universally celebrated. As Jesus says in Matthew 7:9, "You parents—if your children ask for a loaf of bread, do you give them a stone instead?" (NLT). Of course not.

Real-life communities, scientifically speaking, are groups of people who share certain core beliefs and values and live close to one another. They are loving neighbors who routinely help one another without necessarily expecting payback.

The best among Christian churches of the first century AD exemplified ideal communities. In Acts 2:44–45, we're told, "All who believed were together and held everything in common, and they began selling their property and possessions and distributing the proceeds to everyone, as anyone had need" (NET).

Real-life societies, by contrast, are large, spread-out populations of people united by certain overarching values and beliefs, but who belong to diverse races, religions, and political parties. Societies usually comprise a lively mixture of communal and exchange relationships, resulting in everything from heroic altruism to wanton greed.

Today, the Web brings together perfect strangers from opposite sides of the planet. As such, the virtual world is dominated by exchange relationships. Teenagers, for instance, have scores of online "friends" whom they've never met in person, but who expect reciprocity. If they "like" your posts on Instagram, they expect you to like theirs in return—and to exchange likes on Snapchat and Twitter as well. If you don't play along, you run the risk of being—*gasp!*—"unfriended" or "unfollowed."

In other words—and please note this carefully—the main danger of social-media relationships is not the great distance between people. It's the shallowness of the interactions between them. These superficial transactions drown out the relatively few online communal connections we witness, mostly on charitable websites.

The main danger of social-media relationships is not the great distance between people. It's the shallowness of the interactions between them.

Let me illustrate this all-important point by taking you back to Cornell with me.

Even though I knew absolutely no one in upstate New York, even though the campus was deserted because I arrived before the fall semester, and even though the insults from that hardhearted professor were painful, I thrived, thanks in great part to a particularly beautiful blessing I received from my mom. At the end of a long day at the lab, on my way back to my tiny dorm room, I made it a point to stop by the mailroom. Invariably, even before I finished dialing the combination, I could see a solitary letter through the mailbox's little window.

When I reached in and drew out the missive, then looked at the return address, without fail it was from Mom. What's more, the white envelope was almost always edged in red and blue, indicating—for you readers who are too young to remember— that she had sent the letter by airmail.

Every single day.

Seven days a week.

I received a letter from Mom.

That's family.

That's community.

Tragically, that's also what's going the way of the dinosaurs. Consider these few sobering statistics that speak volumes:

- Young people worldwide maintain an average of 8.2 different social-media accounts at once—Instagram being their favorite.[4] In most cases, that's far more than the number of people in their immediate families.
- The average person spends 2.25 hours per day just on social media and Web messaging.[5] Altogether, teens spend north of *nine hours a day* on electronic media of all kinds. That's more than half of their waking lives.[6]
- Many social-media executives are now coming forward and publicly voicing their alarm at what is happening. Recently, Chamath Palihapitiya, a former VP at Facebook, told a Stanford University audience that he feels "tremendous guilt" for helping to create the famous company. "I think," he said, "we have created tools that are ripping apart the social fabric of how society works."[7]

I'm sure you're seeing for yourselves this ruinous phenomenon. My wife, our iGen son, and I certainly are.

A few Novembers back, we decided to change things up for the holidays. We drove from Los Angeles, where we were living at the time, and checked into a resort hotel in Phoenix, Arizona, famous for its Thanksgiving dinners. We invited a young pastor friend to join us. When the big day came, we all dressed up and filed into the giant ballroom, where we beheld long serving tables draped in white tablecloths and loaded with dish upon dish of tasty-looking food. Off to the side, on a small stage, a string quartet serenaded scores of guests sitting and feasting at large round tables.

As I slowly ate my way through the multicourse meal—from cold jumbo shrimp to succulent turkey and all the fixings to pecan pie that was to die for—I kept glancing at one of the nearby tables. It was occupied by a father, mother, and three kids who hardly spoke to one another. The kids were too preoccupied with their smartphones, without any apparent protestations from the parents!

Even though my mother and I were separated by three thousand miles during my time at Cornell, we were closer to one another than the members of that all-too-typical modern American family. Is it the smartphones' fault? Is it social media's fault?

Before you answer, let me ask you this: If Mom and I hadn't had a strong, loving communal relationship, would you have blamed the postal service for it? No!

Honestly, today's Web-wide tragedy is *our* fault. Yes, smartphones and social media facilitate shallow exchange relationships, but we are to blame for falling prey to them. If we all worked harder to nurture communal relationships—not just with our families and best friends but with everyone (yes, everyone)—social media would look very different than it does right now.

In other words, if we ever successfully transformed social media into communal media, it would be a truly marvelous achievement. It would look more like my mother and me exchanging letters. Arguably, it would be the greatest, most selfless achievement in history since Jesus wept and died for us two millennia ago.

So next time you're tempted to shake your fist at social media, remember it isn't technology that is threatening to do us in. It's our misuse of it that clouds our future.

Science and Christianity promote the belief that we are all related genetically and spiritually to one another. That we are all members of one extraordinary species, one divinely created family. According to research, families, in turn, are the most powerful, cohesive elements of healthy communities. And loving, selfless communities are the essential elements of healthy societies. They're all interlinked.

This means we parents, grandparents, and guardians at home have a golden opportunity—no, an obligation—to teach our young charges how to use social media to help others, not to hurt them. To lift up one another, not just ourselves. To unfriend our dark natures and befriend our better angels.

For if we do that, one of humanity's most beautiful commandments, the Golden Rule, will go viral. And consequently, our families, communities, and societies—our entire world—will become more communal than ever before.

Today, consider what community you can be a part of. Unfriend shallow exchanges and opt in for spending face time with the people who really love and care for you and your future. And then share that love with those who have need of a touch of encouragement in their lives. Instead of "likes" on your social-media platforms, you'll receives "loves" in your heart.

23

God's Moral Compass

THE COMMUNITY OF EDUCATION

By Iris O'Brien

One of the most influential communities in our society today is the world of education. It has the power to create the next leaders, visionaries, inventors, scholars, producers, musicians, and teachers. It has the power to mold culture, the family, and our future. Yet with all this influence and opportunity, there exists an even greater challenge in our current educational model.

While there are bright spots in the private school system, the public education system, where the vast majority of our children are being taught, guided, and inspired, is in need of radical transformation. Our method of teaching hasn't changed since the Industrial Revolution and has become a dated, inefficient, bureaucratic dinosaur.

Similar to what has happened in our political system and manufacturing industries, the current public education system lost sight and understanding of its consumer decades ago. And like those two other systems, education is at a crossroads: Either it will foster true intellectual discourse and a traditionally liberal interpretation of being "generous" with our knowledge, or it will sink into a morass of moral despair and intellectual dishonesty fueled by politically correct agendas, post-truth nonsense, and a handful of self-proclaimed social engineers advocating anti-free-speech agendas.

How did we get from being the most innovative society on earth to where we are today? To answer that we must start at the nascent stages of our country's founding and follow influential undercurrents of thought from then to now.

From the mid-1600s to the mid-1800s, public schools as we know them today were nonexistent. Really, the public school is a rather new educational model. During that two-hundred-year period, a child's education was in the hands of communities of family, church, and the free market. You may think this produced illiterate adults, but consider that at this time in history, America produced generations of educated and very highly skilled citizens who laid the foundation for a new nation. If you read the letters and writings of those who lived during this time, you will find that their use of the English language is almost poetic, shaming most written pieces of today's children and adults.

These common citizens were also visionaries who instilled into their children principles of faith, freedom, and self-government like none that had existed before. Today, we all are the beneficiaries of their sacrifice and vision, which reached beyond the self-aggrandizing postures and sense of entitlement of many of our current leaders and young people.

During this time frame in early America, the Bible was the single most important cultural influence in the lives of its citizens. Regardless of whether one was an adherent of the beliefs in the Bible, most everyone recognized that contained within its pages was a treasure trove of truth, wisdom, literary style, and historical fact. It inspired within readers a genuine sense of the need to look beyond oneself to the concept of the greater good to make this country function. Moreover, it set the tone for civility, rule of law, a need for authority, and all that was necessary for attaining to the freedoms we all take for granted.

The Bible was also the cornerstone of the early American education construct as seen through the lens of the truth found in Psalm 127:3 that "children are a heritage from the LORD." As such, parents then believed it was their responsibility not only to teach their children how to make a living, but also how to live. A well-run and high-functioning society is comprised of well-run and high-functioning citizens. Doesn't take a rocket scientist to see that correlation.

Education, then, was not initially a responsibility of government, but the responsibility of the community of family. It really did take a village to raise a child.

In their Bibles, our founding fathers also found the principles that would become the foundation for defining that the existence and function of government was to protect life and property. These principles eventually found their way into our Declaration of Independence as "Life, Liberty and the pursuit of Happiness."[8] Notice that it does not include education.

History has shown that this moral compass of Scripture and the principles that formed the backbone of the freedoms we enjoy today were instrumental in creating intelligent, strong, and solid citizens who created loving and caring communities. The leaders, visionaries, inventors, scholars, mothers, and fathers who were born and educated during this time frame apart from public education can be credited with shaping the society that birthed the greatest personal freedoms on earth. In short, the Bible was the community wellspring that gave definition to the moral compass guiding its culture-shaping members.

As French historian Alexis de Tocqueville observed in *Democracy in America*, America's greatness was a result of the righteousness he saw and heard extolled in the American pulpits. Something helped forge our early national resolve, and it wasn't something people learned in the school system. Let me say that again. *It was not public education that made America great.* It wasn't around to do so.

Another key component to the establishment of the American foundation of these newly defined freedoms was the biblical principle that advocated the innately held belief that human life is the most valuable gift ever given. This value of life fostered a profound honoring of other human beings.

The early definers of the American freedom narrative drew from these biblical principles to create their esteeming of life tone throughout the Declaration of Independence. They spoke of "decent respect to the opinions of mankind" when talking separation from England. They declared their belief in the goodness and equality of humanity: "We hold these truths to be self-evident, that all men are created equal, that they are endowed by their Creator with certain unalienable Rights."[9] Thus they defined the moral compass.

In their declaration of liberty, with the respect for life, they took the high moral ground to state unequivocally that without guaranteeing life, there are no further rights of liberty, freedom, or happy pursuits to enjoy.

This common belief in the intrinsic value of life forged communities that also understood their civic responsibilities, along with the knowledge that freedom comes only with sacrifice. You cannot have one without the other. These morally based communities taught their citizens to honor and respect all people, not just those who were like them. They taught their children that there was a higher authority that we humans answer to; otherwise, life can get too capricious when we choose to respect one day and murder the next. If we're indeed made in the image of our Creator, we have a reason to respect and value each unique individual, no matter the differences.

To yield to a supreme authority is a powerful force that protects us from harm. It frees us to be human. To think otherwise makes us think that we are gods, in charge and in control of our own destinies.

As our nation grew, the inseparability of the Christian ethic from education, whether public or private, was evident at every level of American education. The motto Harvard adopted in 1692 was "Veritas Christo et Ecclesiae," which translated from Latin means "Truth for Christ and the Church." Almost all Ivy League schools and institutions of higher education were created on this same belief system. And again, you did not have to believe in the God of the Bible to benefit from its truths that could be enjoyed by everyone. Freedom is available equally to the Bible-believing citizen as it is to the citizen who is an atheist. And everyone in between.

Unfortunately, faith's influence on education would dramatically decrease during the 1800s. Parents began to leave their homes to work in factories during the Industrial Revolution, opening a door for a new universal thinking that swept the educational system. Local communities naively embraced the model that would ultimately change the American culture, including its educational foundation.

The blueprint of the American public education system was imported from Prussia under the influence of a Progressive named Horace Mann. His scholastic model stemmed less from a belief in the economic and moral needs of free education for all children but more from a desire to create a liberal, tolerant, civilized society. Mann grew up during the early nineteenth century in Massachusetts, where religious tension between Protestants and Catholics dominated life. In his mind, religious schools reinforced these divisions.

The Prussian model, on the other hand, was designed to build a singular national identity, teaching children blind obedience to authority. Applied in America, Mann thought, large groups of students learning together would help to blur the distinctions among members of these divisive religious groups and establish a more egalitarian society. In his own words, "Society should leave the teaching of faith and values to the home and the church and leave the teaching of facts to the school."

Unfortunately, however noble Mann may have intended for his newly advocated system to work, the modern education system was taken over by secular humanists, who totally changed the cultural narrative in education. They stripped out the notion of a God who created men and women with a distinct design and purpose, loves them, and therefore gives all life meaning and value.

They purposely began to indoctrinate children against the existence of a moral authority; they taught them that truth and absolutes don't exist. This agenda reshaped our society, and we are paying the price for it today. We have eliminated the highest possible principles of good in society and lowered the ceiling for what is acceptable. A lost, confused, and chaotic society as we know it today has been the natural result of a worldview of no boundaries. This has contributed to the separation of individuals rather than true engagement that unites.

And statistics in our daily news bear this out: Disillusioned youth who see suicide as the only escape from their disillusionment, random acts of mass violence, apathy, illiteracy, addiction, large-scale divorce, and corporate greed are at all-time highs. Without a moral high ground as our plumb line of accountability, there is no one or nothing to say what is right or wrong.

In this post-truth world, people discard or disregard facts, and truth is totally subjective. I now can make up my own truth. It should come as no surprise that the *Oxford Dictionary's* new word for 2016 was *post-truth* (adjective): "Relating to or denoting circumstances in which objective facts are less influential in shaping public opinion than appeals to emotion and personal belief."[10] The trend toward "post-truth" is more than disturbing.

In this post-truth world, people discard or disregard facts, and truth is totally subjective. I now can make up my own truth.

Can we simply make up what is true? Or decide there is no real truth other than what we deem true, on any given day, swayed by our circumstances, our moods, or a new interest? Is this really the way we want to teach children about the world? Can math, engineering, or science exist without absolute truth? All these disciplines must rely on that which is unchangeable to make what they do work. Why must absolute truth exist for everything in the physical realm but not in the spiritual one?

The modern viewpoint of "post-truth" forges a new version of community that is ultimately destructive, not redemptive. Its principles ultimately create a selfish environment of loving oneself above others and seeking one's own personal good above the greater good. The current cultural narrative is that each of us represents our own higher authority where we decide which life has value and which one may not, whether or not liberty is to be esteemed, and whether freedom is worth the cost and the responsibilities that come with it.

By disavowing moral absolutes, the modern education community has been instrumental in allowing the disintegration of truth in our culture. It has collectively worked with our government to disengage families from effectively training their children to live life with a moral compass, thus giving them marginal and protective boundaries. The belief system of our founding fathers, who created the documents extolling the most revered system of governance ever assembled, has been tossed aside as outdated and irrelevant. The hubris of our current leaders and educators is appalling.

The glaring question we must all ask ourselves is not whether we are better off financially or technologically or educationally, but morally and civilly. Simply, are we better people?

Or are we simply more unhappy and fearful people with better conveniences?

The moral compass found in the Bible gives a framework to life and true education—and a purpose to freedom that everyone can embrace. It shows us how to live in true community with each other and establishes both personal and cultural boundaries teaching the difference between good and evil. It creates a world of redeeming grace that teaches us to serve the greater good by loving others as we love ourselves.

All this is best done through community in loving and honest relationships that was best synthesized when Jesus said, "'Love the Lord your God with all your heart and with all your soul and with all your strength and with all your mind'; and, 'Love your neighbor as yourself'" (Luke 10:27).

Jesus pointed to Himself as the embodiment of the truth that would set us free (John 8:32). This truth that gives us the ability to confidently see and love ourselves from God's perspective as we seek to love Him back and love others as well. This is what everyone in our culture hungers to see.

We must re-engage the national narrative about what is true. This is most needed in the community of educators who will speak up for truth, moral authority, and missing absolutes. Education is the foundation on which our culture is built; as such, it should be the training ground for hope, brilliance, optimism, innovation, and love. The simple truth is this: Education is not something confined to a schoolhouse or an institution. It's more often than not the result of family and community involvements. That is where real education happens and where truth can flourish. Absolutely.

God's Moral Compass

Today, unfriend the forces that seek to strip away the opportunity for truthful exchange between its citizens. Resist the social engineers who want to obliterate the moral pathways that enabled this nation to achieve foundations of freedom and personal welfare never before realized by a nation's citizens.

24

Of Service and Sacrifice

THE COMMUNITY OF HOPE

By Delilah

Religion that God our Father accepts as pure and fault-
less is this: to look after orphans and widows in their
distress and to keep oneself from being polluted by the
world. (James 1:27)

It seems that we are more connected, yet lonelier and more iso-
lated than ever before. Why? Good question. Great question. I
have some ideas.

Never before have we lived in such self-inflicted isolation.
We are placing so much emphasis on the individual that we've

become, in large part, an egocentric society in the United States, and our consumerist approach to life is spreading to become a global phenomenon.

Ask yourself, at what time did a child having his or her "own" bedroom become the norm? I shared a bedroom with a sibling until I left home at eighteen. From there I shared apartments and houses with roommates. I married and had a child. I've never lived by myself. Isn't that normal?

The desire now is for children to have their own room and private dorm quarters, to live in apartments alone, delay marriage, and delay childbirth (until, yes, that child can have a room of *its* own). In this new view of success, where does one learn to get along with others? To solve conflict? To work toward common goals?

Add to this a disconnect with our natural world. We crossed over from a primarily agrarian society to being overwhelmingly urban dwellers some sixty years ago. Initially, folks like my grandparents, who left their five-hundred-acre farm to come to work in the then-lucrative timber trade, still grew most of their own food in the 1950s. My parents had a small veggie garden for many years, but gave it up before I was in high school because the food supply in the United States became so good.

Unfortunately, that means three generations now have grown up not knowing where food comes from—we think it's the supermarket, of course! (Have you noticed that even whole vegetables with roots and leaves are becoming less and less common? Everything is cleaned, peeled, sliced, or chopped and put in sanitary little bags or plastic containers.) The very acts that were needed to keep oneself alive since the beginning when God created the earth and the heavens are being forgotten. This can't bode well for our society.

Why do I bring this into the conversation? Because correcting it requires a group effort—a community.

Many have become so disconnected from life that life itself has lost its meaning and value to them. Depression and anxiety are symptoms suffered in increasing numbers. Do you suppose those who rose before sunrise, did chores before breakfast, worked physically the whole day through, and then tumbled into bed exhausted every night suffered from depression? Ah, the good old days. No, I don't suggest going back to this time period—of course not—but I do think we need to find some balance.

My chores as a kid seemed endless. Laundry, including sorting, washing, drying, folding, ironing, and putting away for six people. Setting and clearing the table; washing, drying, putting away dishes; wiping down the stove and the oven; cleaning out the sink; and sweeping the floor—these were shared by all children every single night without a thought. No dishwasher, no exceptions. Yard work on the weekends as well as splitting and bringing in wood. Veggies were planted and needed to be weeded. Waxing and polishing the hardwood floors once a year. Beds made each morning. You get my drift.

While we certainly grumbled, none of these tasks were too difficult or dangerous to take away from the pleasure of life. It did, however, give purpose. It was our first lesson on what it meant to be part of a community. Community begins at home.

We played for hours with neighbor kids unsupervised, every day. We took risks and pushed boundaries, testing ourselves and our limits, but not those big enough to knowingly get us in real trouble with our folks. We fought and made up without adult interference. Conflict resolution is learned through play.

We were encouraged to join community groups, and we were all anxious to! Brownies, 4-H, Girl Scouts, Rainbow Girls, candy stripers, school clubs, church groups, all of which comprised some form of volunteerism and community outreach. Our society was community minded.

What's my point? The overall "disconnectedness" of people during the last two decades, according to my meter, has taken on a life of its own. I say my meter because I have, for nearly forty years now, taken calls from my listening audience, and I can tell you, the tenor has changed. People seem far, far lonelier.

Family lives are harried, overscheduled, and full of stress. Children have few to zero chores in most homes not because there is nothing to do, but because parents are too pooped to patrol. Play is often reduced to competitive activities that are coached and refereed. Free time is spent in front of a screen. Family time is in front of a screen. School time is in front of a screen.

The me-me-me lifestyle doesn't appear to have led to the bolstering of self-esteem and personal identity. Rather, it has led to questioning the value of one's own life, the devaluation of all life, and the loss of community and connectedness to something greater than one's self.

I have a very difficult time just sitting back and sighing, "Oh well." I'm a self-professed meddler. My meddling led me to found an NGO called Point Hope. Its mission is to raise awareness and champion the cause of forgotten children, especially those in foster care in the United States and West Africa, so that every child has basic essentials to live a healthy life and the opportunity to grow in a loving and nurturing environment. We believe in partnering with individuals, organizations, and companies. One person at a time can change the world for at least one other person—we have seen it happen!

Here in the United States, Point Hope works with children in our very broken foster care system. There are roughly half a million children in foster care, with the average age being eight years old. Only around 22 percent are ever adopted into forever families. That leaves close to four hundred thousand kids hanging in the balance. Their stories are not for the fainthearted. We have a number of programs that support these children. Our Totes of Hope, Beanies for Babies, Point Hope Teenestas, Point Hope Hoorahs, and Points of Hope are all ways that the community can get involved to help.

In Africa, where I was called to work in 2004, it's common for half a dozen people to live in small, unfurnished huts or cinderblock rooms perhaps twelve feet by twelve feet in size. Trust me when I say they never seem lonely, or even depressed, despite their impoverished existence. But they are lacking in the most basic of human needs.

Children work from the time they take their first steps, alongside siblings, parents, grandparents, aunties, and uncles. These aren't the chores of my childhood; they are often fraught with real danger. Life is tasks, and yet they find remarkable joy. They know they play an important role in keeping their family safe, well, and fed. If they sat back on their haunches, they would not eat. It's a pretty powerful motivator. We are nearly devoid of this reality in the Western world. Yet is the African experience a utopian existence? Hardly.

Death is all too common. Infants die, children die, and parents die—from illness, injury, malnourishment, or exposure. But family and community runs strong. It's everything because without it the already fragile dance of life becomes even more precarious.

My mission started in a refugee camp in Ghana, West Africa, where Liberians had fled a bloody regime and the United Nations (UN) had promised a safe harbor. Years passed and some returned, only to be forced out again. Liberia was now supposedly "safe," but its infrastructure had been destroyed; second and third generations had been born in the camp and knew no other home. The UN had pulled out and Ghana wanted them gone. They had no place to go. The result was sixty thousand Liberian refugees living on 140 acres, equipped at its peak to handle four thousand. It was dirty, crime filled, and lacked clean water, food sources, and every basic necessity.

Point Hope has saved countless lives, and brought clean water, sanitation, nutritional and agricultural programs, schools for children, and women's training to these refugees. At the core of our mission is gardening. We teach organic, sustainable gardening practices so that we are not giving handouts and creating more dependencies. We are teaching skill sets to propel people out of poverty and back into self-sustainability. We've barely begun.

I believe we must save ourselves from the existential crisis we are in today through service to others and the use of our bodies and brains.

I live between two worlds so vastly different from another—one of abundance and privilege and one of scarcity and deprivation.

I feel an intense desire to be able to mix and match the good of both, hoping to eliminate the bad. I don't believe everything is bleak, and that "kids these days" are any different from kids of any day. I do believe we need to put a lot more thought and energy into creating a balance. We need to get back to teaching real-life skill sets that used to be part of every school curriculum: home economics, wood shop, electronics. Let's reintroduce the concept of helping ourselves by helping others. Let's conscientiously slow down, unplug, and breathe. We need to sing, dance, and laugh.

Greatness can be found in service. People who aspire to be truly great are those who are the servants of the vulnerable, the helpers of humanity. I believe we must save ourselves from the existential crisis we are in today through service to others and the use of our bodies and brains. We must realign ourselves with our natural world, the cycles of the earth, and God's Word. We must honor the Father and care for one another, as we are all His children.

> Do not be deceived: God cannot be mocked. A man reaps what he sows. Whoever sows to please their flesh, from the flesh will reap destruction; whoever sows to please the Spirit, from the Spirit will reap eternal life. (Galatians 6:7–8)

It's time to redesign our gardens into those that seek a more bountiful harvest of community and hope. Plant yourself in the life of another and be astounded at the fruit you will bear. Unfriend the day-to-day drudgery of self-service and disconnection and find true life in sacrifice and service.

25

Love and Innocence Lost

THE SHADOW COMMUNITY

By Donna Rice Hughes

Human beings are all born with the basic human need to be loved and to love. It's ingrained in our physical, mental, emotional, and spiritual DNA because it was placed there by our Creator. The need to belong and be loved is summed up by Jesus of Nazareth in the greatest commandment: "Love God with all of your heart, mind, soul, body and spirit, and your neighbor as yourself" (see Luke 10:27).

But what happens when children and adults alike look for love, affirmation, and identity by means of "virtual unreality"— digital connections often initiated by and with perfect strangers?

With a plethora of social and virtual communities and instant communications in social media, online gaming systems, chat rooms, and through instant messaging and texting, searching to get these innate human needs met in this intangible, digital world presents a host of challenges that comes with many pitfalls.

Initially, technology was fundamentally neutral, being used for both good and evil purposes. Now, however, Silicon Valley experts like former Google engineer Tristan Harris told *60 Minutes* during an interview that companies have a "whole playbook of techniques" including highly engineered sounds, clicks and ringtones, and colors and designs to keep people compulsively attached to their technology and connected to their virtual worlds.[11] Former Facebook president Sean Parker criticized the social networking giant, saying it is intentionally "exploiting a vulnerability in human society" and "literally changes your relationship with society, with each other."[12]

When people spend more time looking at their screen than at each other in their physical world, it's a red flag to take a technology break.

The digital world that promised to bring us together in true community, relationship, and acceptance has, in many instances, created greater separation, isolation, depression, lack of empathy, false security, counterfeit sex, anonymous interactions with strangers, and dangerous and even deadly encounters. Relationships formed in the digital world have come to represent a connected and woven marketing Web often fueled by "likes," "shares," and "retweets" instead of solid relationships and friendships based on mutual respect, dignity, and civility. Our tendency to replace face-to-face interactions with virtual interactions may be sabotaging our ability to get our love needs met.

A boundaryless internet has shrunk our world and allows instant communications in seconds with people around the world. Close, meaningful relationships with online connections become difficult to maintain, and, ironically, often pull time, attention, and physical connections away from family and friends in our immediate circles. When people spend more time looking at their screen than at each other in their physical world, it's a red flag to take a technology break.

Never has the dysfunctional downside of the digital world been more apparent and evidenced than in the pandemic of cyberbullying and internet pornography. Both lead to brokenness in different ways.

The CyberWorld Begets the CyberBully

In the offline world, communities are typically responsible for enforcing norms of privacy, general etiquette, and the security of boundaries of family, church, and trusted friends within the "village" of community. Unfortunately, true community in which brotherly love thrives is sadly compromised on many levels in a 24/7, digital world.

In the digital world, where by definition communities are virtual and abstract by nature, children and young adults become dependent on and addicted to instant community, instant response, and instant celebrity. They have access to real-time and asynchronous communication features; blogging tools;

photo-, music-, and video-sharing features; and the ability to post original creative work—all linked to a unique profile that can be customized and updated on a regular basis.

Social-media forums allow kids to present themselves to the world, seek approval from their peers, describe their interests, connect with others, jockey for status, and seek validation and affirmation. Conversely, they may also post risqué pictures, brag about the previous weekend's adventures and conquests, and use this digital space to humiliate others or post inappropriate content.

Cyberbullying was nonexistent before the interactive nature of social media gave birth to this epidemic, one of the many black marks of the Web 2.0 era. Cyberbullies can threaten or destroy the reputation of another while hiding behind the protective barrier of a laptop screen or smartphone. The technology itself creates a barrier that can block true empathy, in turn setting up a perfect environment for bullying behaviors to thrive. It has been reported that nearly half of young people (47 percent) have received intimidating, threatening, or nasty messages online.[13] Further, girls (40.6 percent) are much more likely to be victims of cyberbullying than boys (28.8 percent).[14] Girls also dominate social media, while boys tend to play video games.

The impact of cyberbullying is vast, having been linked to depression, anxiety, increased feelings of sadness and loneliness, changes in sleep and eating patterns, loss of interest in activities, and, in the most tragic cases, suicide.

In the absence of a personal, face-to-face interaction—an essential encounter where one learns to communicate, interact, solve differences, play by the rules, grow, and learn—it's no wonder that kids have such a difficult time developing healthy friendships and relationships, and learning to respect and relate to members of the opposite sex.

A Pornified Culture

In 1994, the internet exploded with the new distribution vehicle for what was once black-market pornography and child pornography. Many of the laws that were passed to prevent this weren't upheld by an ignorant Supreme Court. And the laws that are in place have either not been adequately enforced or completely ignored, as in the case of federal obscenity statutes. This toxic, "pornified" culture pushes the cheap, lust-filled counterfeit of genuine erotic love. It's everywhere, it's coarse, and it's graphic. Pornographic messages promote taking rather than giving: "You exist for my pleasure. You are a sex object. You are valued for your body parts and not for your heart and personhood. Once I am done with you, you are expendable."

True erotic love of genuine intimacy designed by God to be enjoyed on a physical, emotional, mental, and spiritual level has been counterfeited by the instant gratification through internet pornography, virtual sexual encounters, sexting, and the ugly pornographic counterpart of cyberbullying: revenge porn.

Current medical and social science confirms that pornography harms children, women, men, marriages, and the culture at large. It is the drug of this millennium, fueling sex addiction, deviant sex practices, sexual exploitation, and abuse of women and children, and the multibillion-dollar sex-trafficking industry. It's exploitative, and often violent and deviant. The invasion of graphic online pornography worldwide is "the largest unregulated social experiment in human history"[15] and is a hidden public-health hazard. Pornography is "deforming the sexual development of young viewers."[16] Statistics don't lie:

88.2 percent of top-rated porn scenes contain physical aggression (spanking, gagging, slapping, etc.); 48.7 percent contain verbal aggression (name calling). Perpetrators were usually male; 94 percent of the targets were women.[17] Searches for "teen porn" tripled 2005 to 2013.[18]

Our bodies were made for God-given and God-modeled love, for "becoming one" with another in marriage (1 Corinthians 6:18–20). In this pervasive pornified digital culture, where women and children are objectified, used, abused, and sold for sex, true love is taken out of the equation and replaced instead with selfish acts of lust, sexual exploitation, and, in many cases, complete disregard of God's creation. How can we expect children to model love, have healthy relationships, and form positive and loving thoughts about others when they are exposed to unprecedented rates of online pornography offering the exact opposite message?

Internet attraction that creates community dysfunction plays into the world you live in—destructive relationships leading to the pandemic of objectification and sexual exploitation that plays out in sex trafficking and more.

The Message that Matters

In Paul's letter to the Colossians, he tells believers to "put on love" over all other virtues (forgiveness, bearing one another). Putting on love takes courage. It does mean having to say you're sorry, putting yourself in another's shoes, showing compassion, sacrificing for others, loving your enemies, and serving the greater good. It's not about taking but about giving. In Scripture, God beckons humans to love Him and our neighbors as ourselves, embracing real, genuine, sacrificial love—love that puts others first.

Jesus ramped up the first commandment with what pastor Andy Stanley calls the "platinum rule," to love others as He has loved us, which means totally, unconditionally, and sacrificially, expecting nothing in return.

For the sake of our children, we need to create an online epidemic of kindness and civility in a digital world rampant with hate, division, cyberbullying, and sexual exploitation. Unfriend digital degradation and perversion in favor of a culture of human dignity and respect. Let's begin to build a community that represents a godly culture of love.

Notes

1   "Declaration of Independence: A Transcription," National Archives, https://www.archives.gov/founding-docs/declaration-transcript. Historically, the term men has been used generically to denote both men and women. Contrary to politically correct propaganda, diversity did not start with political correctness.

2   Robert Puff, "Two Key Steps to Finding Happiness," *Psychology Today*, May 9, 2012, https://www.psychologytoday.com/us/blog/meditation -modern-life/201205/two-key-steps-finding-happiness.

3   "Definition of Transparent in US English," Oxford University Press, https://en.oxforddictionaries.com/definition/us/transparent.

4   "GlobalWebIndex," GWI Social, 2017, https://cdn2.hubspot.net/hubfs /304927/Downloads/GWI%20Social%20Summary%20Q3%202017.pdf.

5   "GlobalWebIndex," GWI Social.

6   Hayley Tsukayama, "Teens Spend Nearly Nine Hours Every Day Consuming Media," Washington Post, November 3, 2015, https://www. washingtonpost.com/news/the-switch/wp/2015/11/03/teens-spend -nearly-nine-hours-every-day-consuming-media/?utm_term=.b98c 7d53c815.

7   James Vincent, "Former Facebook Exec Says Social Media Is Ripping Apart Society," The Verge, December 11, 2017, https://www.theverge. com/2017/12/11/16761016/former-facebook-exec-ripping-apart-society.

8   "Declaration of Independence: A Transcription," National Archives.

9   "Declaration of Independence: A Transcription," National Archives.

10 "Definition of Post-Truth in US English," Oxford University Press, https://en.oxforddictionaries.com/definition/post-truth.

11 "Why Can't We Put Down Our Smartphones?" CBS News, April 7, 2017, https://www.cbsnews.com/news/why-cant-we-put-down-our -smartphones-60-minutes/.

12 Sean Parker, "Facebook takes advantage of 'vulnerability in human psychology,'" CBS News, November 9, 2017, https://www.cbsnews.com

/news/sean-parker-facebook-takes-advantage-of-vulnerability-in
-human-psychology/.

13 "Safety net: The cyberbully inquiry," Children's Society, https://www.
childrenssociety.org.uk/cyberbullying-inquiry.

14 Sameer Hinduja and Justin W. Patchin, "Cyberbullying by Gender,"
Cyberbullying, 2015, https://cyberbullying.org/wp-content/uploads
/2015/05/cyberbullying-gender-20151.jpg.

15 Michael Seto, conversation at the first meeting of the International
Centre for Missing & Exploited Children (ICMEC), Gloram Health
Coalition, Zurich, Switzerland, October 10, 2012. Seto is Director of
Forensic Rehabilitation Research, Royal Ottawa Health Care Group, and
a member of ICMEC.

16 Mary Eberstadt and Mary Ann Layden, "The Social Cost of Pornography:
A Statement of Findings and Recommendations," *The Witherspoon Institute*, 2014, http://www.internetsafety101.org/upload/file
/Social%20Costs%20of%20Pornography%20.

17 Chyng Sun, Ana Bridges, Robert Wosnitzer, et al, "A Comparison of Male
and Female Directors in Popular Pornography: What Happens When
Women Are at the Helm?," *Psychology of Women Quarterly*, vol. 32, no. 3
(2008): 312–325.

18 Gail Dines, "A rare defeat for corporate lobbyists," August 1, 2013),
http://www. counterpunch.org/ 2013/08/01/a–rare–defeat–for–corporate
–lobbyists. Dr. Dines also analyzed the content of the three most popular
"porntubes," the portals that serve as gateways to online porn, and found
that they contained 18 million teen-related pages–again, the largest single genre and about one-third of the total content.

Contributors

Delilah, the most-listened-to woman on radio in the United States, embraced the medium when she was a middle-schooler in Reedsport, Oregon, reporting school news and sports on KDUN-AM, a small station in her hometown. Delilah's soothing voice, open heart, and love of music expanded her audience from the folks in Reedsport to more than 10 million monthly listeners on about 150 radio stations across the United States. Many of those listeners engage Delilah beyond the airwaves via social media, especially on Facebook, where 1.6 million friends connect with her to share their stories and request songs.

Delilah, who celebrated the thirty-year anniversary of her nighttime radio program in 2016 (the program was launched nationally in early 1997), was honored with the radio industry's highest accolade the same year—the NAB Marconi Award for "Network/Syndicated Personality of the Year." She was also inducted in the National Radio Hall of Fame in 2016 and joined the NAB Broadcasting Hall of Fame in 2017, which marked the first time a woman had been honored in the last thirty-five years. In addition to yearly honors by *Radio Ink* as one of the "Most Influential Women in Radio," Delilah took home the trophy for "Outstanding Host – Entertainment/Information" at the Alliance of Women in Media's 37th Annual Gracie Awards Gala.

Delilah's distinctive blend of storytelling, sympathetic

listening, and encouragement—all scored with adult contemporary soft rock—makes her top ranked in most markets among women aged twenty-five to fifty-four. She says her show is a "safety zone where listeners take off their armor, slip into a 'Mr. Rogers' cardigan, sit around the electronic hearth, and share their secrets."

She adds that her audience is "just like me and the two women working on the show, who were once listeners. We are single parents who work hard to strike a balance between family and work life. We also enjoy our friendships and remember to laugh as much as possible."

Often referred to as the "Oprah of Radio," Delilah is also the author of three books, including *Arms Full of Love*, which was released in 2012. Published by Harlequin Books, it features a poignant and emotional collection of heartfelt listener stories and Delilah's own tales that demonstrate the importance of family.

As a mother of thirteen children, ten of whom she adopted, Delilah established a foundation called Point Hope as a voice for forgotten children everywhere. Now in its twelfth year, the immediate focus of the foundation is on refugee children in Ghana and on special needs children in the foster care system nationwide and in her neighborhood of White Center in Seattle. Delilah also recently partnered with Feed the Children, an international nonprofit relief organization that distributes food, medicine, clothing, and other necessities to those in need. Delilah has joined the effort to help provide food and necessities to hungry children in America by raising awareness of the heartbreak of hungry children with her millions of nightly listeners.

In addition to a passion for children and radio, Delilah is devoted to music because "it touches the heart the way nothing else can." Her father had a Country-Western band, and her brother played in a Jazz band. Though she writes lyrics, she cannot sing. Delilah says, "I always wanted to be a performer, but I can't sing, dance, or act. Luckily, I found I could talk!"

Delilah loves her work "because it has allowed me to bring together a distinct community of people who reach out to help one another. We don't try to fix people. We listen. We sympathize. We empathize. If the show has a message, it's listen to your own gut. Trust your own intuition. Go where it leads. Don't give up."

Daily broadcasts, caring for her children, running a foundation, writing books, traveling, and public speaking add up to a very busy life for Delilah. And she wouldn't have it any other way.

Iris O'Brien is a visionary, entrepreneur, trained chef, designer, artist, producer, and writer. She holds a design patent on her Tuscan Oven. Her first career was lived out in Oxmoor House test kitchens. Her second home was where she raised her four children—Ivey, Sage, Jack, and Jorgia—with her husband, Dr. John A. O'Brien.

Iris is a founder and creative director of curriculum development for EPIC (Eternal Perspective Influencing Culture), teaching students to create culture, not follow it. EPIC is a smartphone/iPad application-based curriculum environment that uses blended and project-based learning to teach teens biblical principles, how those principles are relevant in their world, and how to apply them in everyday life. EPIC instills a biblical worldview in children that will empower them to go out and impart an eternal perspective that influences culture.

Iris is the owner of Field of Masters virtual publishing, where she has produced, directed, and published the series *Secrets of a*

Sommelier. She has numerous written books, including *Stairway to Heavenly Thinking, Hope: You Are Not Alone,* and *A Historical Timeline of Wine.* She and her family live in Birmingham, Alabama. For more information, visit epicrelevantlearning.com.

Michael Guillen is a three-time Emmy Award winner, bestselling author, and former Harvard University instructor. Dr. Guillen is known and loved by millions as the ABC News Science Editor, a post he filled for fourteen years (1988–2002). In that capacity, he appeared regularly on *Good Morning America, 20/20, Nightline,* and *World News Tonight.* He is host of *Where Did It Come From?*, a popular one-hour primetime series for The History Channel that debuted in fall 2006.

In association with Anonymous Content, Dr. Guillen produced *Little Red Wagon,* the award-winning motion picture written by Patrick Sheane Duncan (*Mr. Holland's Opus, Courage Under Fire*) and directed by David Anspaugh (*Rudy, Hoosiers*). After playing in theaters nationwide, it became a Walmart bestseller and is now on Netflix.

Dr. Guillen's articles have appeared in publications such as *Science News, Psychology Today, The New York Times,* and *The Washington Post.* He is a columnist for *Fox News, U.S. News & World Report,* and *The Christian Post,* as well as a popular public speaker.

Dr. Guillen is also the bestselling author of *Bridges to Infinity: the Human Side of Mathematics; Five Equations That Changed the World: The Power and Poetry of Mathematics; Can a Smart Person Believe in God?; Amazing Truths: How Science and the Bible Agree;* and his first thriller novel, *The Null Prophecy,* which was released July 2017. He is currently working on a nonfiction book, *The End of the World as We Know It: How Science is Changing Everything*, scheduled for release in October 2018.

A native of East Los Angeles, Dr. Guillen earned his BS from UCLA and his PhD in physics, mathematics, and astronomy from Cornell University. He has received honorary doctorates from the University of Maryland and Pepperdine University. In 2000 he was elected to the renowned, century-old Explorers Club. He is a member of the Writers Guild of America.

Dr. Guillen is president of Spectacular Science Productions Inc. He currently lives in Nashville with his wife, their son, and a growing assortment of barnyard animals. For more information, visit michaelguillen.com.

Donna Rice Hughes, CEO and president of Enough Is Enough® (EIE), is a progressive leader, social entrepreneur, internet safety expert, author, speaker, commentator, and producer. As president of EIE, she is regularly sought out by media, Congress, and industry leaders for her expertise in preventing the sexual exploitation of children online. She's given thousands of media interviews, over four hundred seminars/speeches, and several congressional testimonies. Under her leadership, EIE created the award-winning Internet Safety 101 curriculum for parents and educators in partnership with U.S. Department of Justice.

She developed the historic Children's Internet Safety Presidential Pledge signed by candidate Trump and supported later by candidate Clinton. Awards include an Emmy for the PBS/EIE *Internet Safety 101®* TV series, an Emmy nomination as the program's host (2012), the Women In Technology Award for Social Impact (2013), and the Professional Women in Advocacy Excellence in Advocacy Award for "Veteran Practitioner"

(2014). She has authored *Kids Online: Protecting Your Children In Cyberspace* and numerous articles in mainstream media.

Hughes graduated magna cum laude, Phi Beta Kappa from the University of South Carolina and is married to Jack Hughes. They live in Northern Virginia and have three grandchildren. Find her at enough.org; internetsafety101.org; and donnaricehughes. com.

About the Author

Joe Battaglia is a broadcaster, author (*The Politically Incorrect Jesus, That's My Dad, Fathers Say*), and founder and president of Renaissance Communications, a media company whose mission is to provide media platforms for gifted communicators of biblical truth.

His clients include Dr. Steve Brown and his nationally syndicated radio program *Key Life*, Prison Fellowship, Affirm Films/Sony Pictures Entertainment, Provident Films, Pure Flix Entertainment, actress Shari Rigby, and author and speaker Jeanne Nigro. Joe is also an executive producer and general manager of the nationally syndicated radio program *Keep the Faith,* the number-one, faith-based music radio program in the nation with a weekly audience of over two million.

For over sixteen years, Joe has also been involved in the promotion of highly successful hit movies to the faith-based marketplace, such as *The Passion*; *The Lion, the Witch & the Wardrobe*; *The Polar Express*; *Facing the Giants*; *Fireproof*; *Courageous*; *Soul Surfer*; *Son of God*; *God's Not Dead*; *Heaven Is for Real*; *Miracles from Heaven*; *Risen*; *War Room*; *The Star*; and *I Can Only Imagine.*

Highly active in the Christian music industry, Joe served on the board of Gospel Music Association for twenty years, was chairman of the National Christian Radio Association for fourteen years, and currently sits on the boards of the National Religious Broadcasters and WAY Media.

Prior to forming Renaissance in 1992, Joe was vice president of Communicom Corp. of America, the parent company of WWDJ/New York, WZZD/Philadelphia, and KSLR/San Antonio. He was with Communicom for over eighteen years, eight as general manager of the flagship station WWDJ from 1982–1990. From 1979–1995, he also was a partner in Living Communications, parent company of WLIX/Long Island and WLVX/ Hartford, Connecticut.

In 1991, Joe penned his first book, *A New Suit for Lazarus* (Thomas Nelson). He attended Boston University, graduating magna cum laude with a BS in Journalism. He lives in New Jersey and is the parent of a twenty-nine-year-old daughter, Alanna.